More Praise for *When Growth Stalls*

"This is a must-read for all business leaders. Steve McKee offers real-world examples and insight into why growth stalls, and tells how to overcome the pitfalls that cause it. I couldn't put this book down."

> —Todd Parent, founder and CEO, Extreme Pizza

"Steve McKee brings focused insights and keen observations to bear against a business leader's greatest fear. *When Growth Stalls* is the field manual for those facing the challenge of getting things back on track."

> —Tom McLoughlin, vice president of marketing,
> The Scotts Miracle-Gro Company

"Any business leader planning on sustaining growth for the long term should read this book. It's inevitable that you will experience stalled growth at some point, and this book, based on the author's own experience, provides a realistic approach to overcoming it."

> —Jamie Chilcoff, president and CEO, FiberTech Polymers

"Business stalled? Steve McKee feels your pain because he's been there. McKee lays out well-researched reasons why companies stall—and how you can get yours out of its funk. Written from his heart, it'll lift your soul and your bottom line."

> —Tory Johnson, CEO, Women For Hire

"If your company growth has stalled or if you want to grow faster, this book is the fastest way to find enlightenment."

> —Mike Faith, CEO and president, Headsets.com, Inc.

"For any executive or business leader, the timing of *When Growth Stalls* couldn't be more perfect. McKee provides specific strategies, examples, and ideas for improving and maintaining growth, especially in turbulent times."

> —Tina Sampson, vice president of sales and marketing,
> Gaylord National Resort and Convention Center

"Steve McKee has effectively woven years of research into his personal experience, making *When Growth Stalls* a compelling read, particularly in challenging economic times. We're all worried about stalling out and I finished the book re-charged and fueled with solid information to drive my business's growth."

> —Mark Vengroff, CEO, Vengroff,
> Williams & Associates, Inc.

"By using real-world examples of businesses facing the challenge of stalled growth, McKee makes his principles easy to understand and entertaining for the reader. A particularly timely guide for executives, managers, and entrepreneurs."

> —Ethan Ewing, president, Bills.com

"*When Growth Stalls* is a practical presentation of how marketing-based management principles can contribute to enduring growth. A quick and entertaining read, it cuts through the complexity to focus on solutions and help accelerate the time to renewed growth."

> —Ian Davison, marketing director, Detour Bars

When Growth Stalls

How It Happens, Why You're Stuck,
and What to Do About It

Steve McKee

JOSSEY-BASS
A Wiley Company
San Francisco

Published by Jossey-Bass
A Wiley Imprint
989 Market Street, San Francisco, CA 94103-1741—www.josseybass.com

Jossey-Bass books and products are available through most bookstores. To contact Jossey-Bass directly, call our Customer Care Department within the U.S. at (800) 956-7739, outside the U.S. at (317) 572-3986, or fax (317) 572-4002.

Jossey-Bass also publishes its books in a variety of electronic formats. Some content that appears in print may not be available in electronic books.

Library of Congress Cataloging-in-Publication Data

McKee, Steve, 1963-
  When growth stalls : how it happens, why you're stuck, and what to do about it / Steve McKee.
    p. cm.
  Includes bibliographical references and index.
  ISBN 978-0-470-39570-7 (cloth)
  1. Small business—Growth. 2. Success in business. 3. Business planning. I. Title.
  HD62.7.M395 2009
  658.4'06—dc22   2008051601

Printed in the United States of America
FIRST EDITION
HB Printing   10 9 8 7 6 5 4 3 2 1

Contents

To Denise. Forever.

Acknowledgments

Although only one author's name is on the spine, this book is the result of many people's efforts. I must, of course, begin with Denise, the love of my life, who encourages me to no end. Next come my four wonderful kids—Garvey, Cassidy, Riley, and Delaney—who gave unselfishly of their time when I was hunched over my Mac, thought it was pretty cool that Dad was writing a book, and said that maybe someday they'd even be interested in reading it. (I won't hold my breath.)

I am deeply grateful to my clients, whose continued partnership is the source of stability at McKee Wallwork Cleveland. Without their wisdom and willingness to explore new ground, we would not have accomplished anything. Nor would any of it have been possible without the staff at MWC, whose outstanding talents and capabilities never cease to amaze me and have enabled me to take on this project. That goes especially for Bart Cleveland and Pat Wallwork, the best partners I could ever hope to have.

I am grateful to my good friend, Mark Mathis, who took the authorship plunge first and patiently encouraged me to do the same. Judith Ehrlich has been everything I had hoped for in an agent and gave me wise guidance, including referring me to my gifted editor, Karl Weber, who was of great help in shaping and molding this project (and was so encouraging, even when the pages were full of "tracked changes"). I also want to thank Rebecca Browning, Erin Moy, and the team at Jossey-Bass for believing in the enthusiasm of an unproven author.

Donna Delhagen and Jerry Thomas at Decision Analyst worked very hard on the research and have exhibited a true spirit of partnership through the past five years. They are truly first-rate. Donna Adler took a chance on me when I was a fresh-faced twenty-two-year-old, and without her doing so, who knows where I'd be today. Betsy Hunter and Joseph Olin both provided immeasurable mentorship to me in the early stages of my career, opening my eyes to principles and possibilities that have evolved into my marketing philosophy. And Peter Strascina taught me so much about business—and life—that I can't thank him enough.

I thank my late father, Richard McKee, who was a great example to me, and my mother, Ginni, who still is—and who opened her home to me while she was away, giving me the perfect office-away-from-the-office. Zach Franchini spent the first month of his summer internship saving me from the footnote monster (sorry, Zach, but at least now all those term papers will be easy). And Jon Patten and the crew at Dion's kept me full of brain food and were gracious when my laptop and I repeatedly overstayed our welcome.

Last, I am grateful to everyone at Kinship and the institute for their love and encouragement and to Jesus, who is the source of all good things.

Introduction

I'm always looking for profitable growth on a sustained basis. That's I think the hardest challenge in business— to not do it just once, but year after year.[1]

—*Bruce Carbonari, CEO, Fortune Brands*

One of the toughest lessons every business leader learns is how difficult it is to generate consistent growth. There is always something—or someone—that threatens even the healthiest business model. As a result, stalled growth is the rule, not the exception, even for the best-managed companies.

That's especially true in unpredictable economic environments, when circumstances beyond their control catch business leaders off guard. How they respond to those circumstances makes a big difference to their companies' future prospects.

This book is about generating growth for your company at a time when growth may be nothing but a glimmer of hope in your mind. It offers, first of all, perspective on the external market forces that hinder growth in every organization. It goes on to expose the destructive dynamics that are likely playing out within your company (and of which you may be unaware). Then it offers a set of core principles that can help set you back on the growth path—not a secret formula but a proven pattern that you can apply to your own unique circumstances.

Stalled growth is a phenomenon I've witnessed time and time again over the course of a career spanning more than two decades in the advertising industry. My company, McKee Wallwork Cleveland, is less an advertising agency than it is a consulting firm, and we've built our reputation not by simply making and placing ads but by diagnosing and addressing our clients' most difficult marketing challenges. Sometimes the solutions involve advertising, and sometimes they don't.

Working with clients of all shapes and sizes—and in a variety of industries—has given us a unique perspective on the challenges facing companies that are struggling, stalled, and simply stuck. But it wasn't until we went through a growth crisis of our own and subsequently embarked on a five-year journey of research and discovery that the patterns that are the subject of this book came alive.

When Growth Stalls is the culmination of a journey that for me began in 2003, when after five years of breathtaking growth my firm suddenly and shockingly stalled. The reasons weren't clear, and at first we assumed it was just a blip on our stellar run of continuous revenue increases. But through two painful years of trial and error, we discovered that all of the skills, enthusiasm, and expertise we had were not enough to restart our growth engine.

A funny thing happened, however, on our way downhill. Through our conversations with other companies in similar straits, we discovered that we were not alone. In fact, we had a great deal in common with them. That gave us a hunch that perhaps we could study the problem of stalled growth from a position of objectivity and uncover principles that would get us back on track.

We commissioned two nationwide quantitative studies—the first in 2003, and a second, deeper dive as the mortgage meltdown led to the credit crunch and global economic crisis in 2008—to explore the dynamics that fuel growth, understand the characteristics that cause it to stall, and shed light on the reasons why some companies stay down longer than others. We interviewed CEOs of major corporations and entrepreneurs of every stripe to gain further insight and breathe life into our findings.

We tested the patterns we identified by sharing them with thousands of business leaders facing widely divergent business circumstances in industries as diverse as retail, manufacturing, health care, education, technology, travel, and professional services. And we began applying the principles to our own growth challenges and those of our clients. That gave us a first-person understanding of the impact their applications can have.

Our research has turned our understanding of stalled growth—and our approach to turning it around—literally inside out. We have found that regardless of what's happening outside an enterprise, it's what's inside that counts.

I first began sharing what we learned in an eight-part series for *BusinessWeek.com*. That led to invitations to speak before civic groups, industry trade associations, and corporate retreats. As I shared these principles with group after group, I saw heads nodding in agreement when I described what was happening within their companies without ever having set foot in them. Before I knew it, the message began taking on a life of its own, and I realized we had hit a nerve. There was a bigger story here, and it needed to be told.

Sluggish growth is generally produced not by mismanagement or strategic blundering but by natural market forces and management dynamics that are widespread, often unrecognized, and highly destructive. And there are seven characteristics that are most commonly to blame.

Three may not be surprising. They are external forces to which countless companies have fallen victim: economic upheavals, aggressive competition, and changing industry dynamics. What was so fascinating to learn, however, is how often they catch company leaders off guard. These factors do a lot of damage simply by going unrecognized for too long.

More surprising are four subtle and highly destructive internal factors that conspire to keep companies down: lack of consensus among the management team, loss of focus, loss of nerve, and marketing inconsistency. All four are psychological, all are capable of ruining companies from the inside out, and all are preventable—*if* you know what to look for. We found that most struggling companies suffer from some combination of these seven factors.

If your company is currently struggling, *When Growth Stalls* may be just what you need to shake things up. It will cut through some of the confusion and doubt that may be cluttering your mind and will help you recognize that the challenges you're facing are neither unique nor insurmountable. For those whose growth picture looks rosy—for the time being—gaining a better understanding of the dangerous dynamics *every* company eventually faces may be just what you need to avoid the growth meltdown waiting around the corner.

My company had to learn these lessons the hard way. It is my hope that the insights shared on the following pages will be as valuable to you as they have been to me.

When Growth Stalls

1

It's Not Just Business, It's Personal

A lush green jewel of the southern California desert, Rancho Mirage is a beautiful place, but it's not easy to reach. After a smooth and uneventful flight via jumbo jet to Phoenix, my wife and I caught a connection on an old propeller plane that would take us across the Mojave desert into the Palm Springs airport, where a shuttle would take us to the resort where we were staying. Unfortunately, it was a warm springtime afternoon, and the thermals caused our slow, small aircraft to shake and shudder all the way there. The plane landed long before our stomachs did.

The bumpy ride was an apt metaphor. As president of McKee Wallwork Cleveland Advertising, I was heading to the annual Inc. 500 Conference to take a bow on behalf of the company, which had been recognized as one of the fastest-growing private businesses in America. It was quite an honor. The award is based on growth achieved over the course of not just one year but five years. A company can't make the list based on a single big win or one hot season; it has to demonstrate growth *and* sustainability. And we had, at least for now.

I had been in the advertising business for just over a decade when we launched the company. My career had been a whirlwind to that point. I had worked at four different agencies, including a giant multinational, a creative hot shop, and a closely held boutique. I'd climbed a steep learning curve, using each opportunity to broaden my knowledge and deepen my understanding of the advertising industry.

Not that it was easy. During my first few months in the business, I would sit in meetings and pray that no one would call on me because I didn't know what they were talking about. Whenever I heard unfamiliar jargon (which happened a lot), I would surreptitiously jot it down in my notebook so I could look it up when I got home that night.

Within about a year, I started feeling comfortable, in part because I'd been studying my field in every way possible. I read *Adweek* and *Advertising Age* cover to cover each week and picked up every marketing book I could find. I paid rapt attention to high-profile advertising campaigns in the marketplace and noted how well they worked (or didn't). I started working backward from ads I saw, challenging myself to figure out the strategy behind them and to try to imagine a better execution. And I began a game inside my head of predicting which campaigns would succeed and which would fail based on what I knew about marketing and consumer behavior. (Call it "fantasy marketing," an ad geek's version of the fantasy football millions of fans play with imaginary team rosters.) More often than not, my guesses proved right, and with each confirmation, my self-confidence grew.

After ten fast-paced years, I'd risen to the position of president at a well-respected regional agency. When my proposed buyout of the firm fell through, I figured I was good enough to strike out on my own. After all, I had been a key contributor to strategies that made a lot of companies successful. Now I wanted to do it for myself.

And the best part was that I wouldn't have to do it alone. Pat Wallwork, a talented Procter & Gamble veteran and media director at the agency where I had previously been president, resigned shortly after I did. She, too, thought she had what it took to make a go of it as an agency principal. Both of us, we later found out, were advised by friends that partnerships rarely work, but we had a gut feeling about each other. So we put together a business plan, rented an office in our hometown of Albuquerque, and launched McKee Wallwork Advertising.

As anyone who has started a company knows, in the early days you have to wear a lot of hats. In addition to her role as media director, Pat did the accounting, and I handled sales as well as account management and creative development. Pat's a morning person and would get to the office as early as 6 or 7AM; as a night person, I would often stay past eight o'clock. We joked that as long as we didn't go to the bathroom at the same time, there would always be someone there to answer the phone. We're both focused, intense people, and we had the added incentive of being in debt with no income. So we put our heads down and went to work.

We immediately picked up a few project accounts; not enough to pay the bills, but enough to give us encouragement and make us feel like we were a real business. Within a couple of months, we landed our first real client and hired our first employee. Then things took off.

We started growing quickly, adding clients and staff, and managing our money conservatively so that we wouldn't have to tap the line of credit we had negotiated with our bank. Five years later, we came up for air and found that we had become one of America's fastest-growing companies. Our initial instincts were correct: we knew what we were doing, we'd built a strong partnership, and we'd made it through the challenging startup phase. Sure, there were bumps along the way, but overall those first five years had been a fast and smooth ride.

But in the months leading up to the Inc. 500 Conference, things started to get bumpier. There was no clear reason for it. Our clients were happy, the economy was stable, and we'd maintained our book of business. Still, our growth had slowed, and it concerned me.

What I didn't realize then was that the uneasiness I was feeling was an early symptom of a more serious problem happening to the firm. Over the next two years, I would gain a deep understanding of the confusion and frustration so many corporate leaders feel when their growth begins to stall. As it turned out, our company's struggle would lead to the research that served as the foundation for this book. It would also make our firm more effective for—and more empathetic to—the struggling clients who now come to us for answers to their growth problems.

At the time, however, I couldn't see any of that coming. All I knew was that I felt odd receiving the plaudits at Rancho Mirage, glad-handing leaders of the nation's most successful companies while wondering whether I had something to hide. Had we made a mistake? Why was this happening to us now? Are we just pretenders? Questions like these nagged me throughout the course of the conference, taking the shine off what should have been a gratifying celebration. But I couldn't help it. I felt like we didn't belong, that maybe our appearance on the list was a mistake.

I didn't know it at the time, but our growth problems would continue throughout the rest of that year. After five years of rapid growth, we ended the year with revenues down nearly 6 percent. We lost a quarter of our staff. And the following year was worse: sales declined another 16 percent, and employee turnover shot up to 67 percent. As a company whose business model was predicated on helping other companies grow, not having our own house in order was, frankly, embarrassing.

What happened?

I now know that it was nothing unusual. Even the best-managed companies experience growth problems that can be mystifying to those on the inside. But at the time, it was ulcer-inducing. I thought we must have really done something wrong.

Companies are interesting social organisms. No matter what kind of face you put on, when something is amiss, everybody can sense it. We had assembled a terrific team and arm in arm set about to conquer the world of advertising, and as things began to slow, our positive psychological momentum continued for a while. But slowly, noticeably, as our growth started running out of gas, I began to see doubt in our employees' eyes. They started to wonder whether all of the promise they had seen early on was anything more than that. They started to worry about their paychecks. That made me even more anxious—and more determined to figure out what ailed our company.

My colleagues and I boiled the challenge down to one simple question: Why would a prospective client look past all the established, reputable agencies on the East and West coasts in favor of a boutique in the emerging Southwest? If we could answer that, we could rekindle the growth to which we had become accustomed.

We'd found that we had done our best work when we could report to decision makers with real skin in the game, who had vision and guts, and who, like us, were thinking about conquering the world rather than simply advancing their own career paths. We saw the benefits of working with companies whose marketing budgets were increasing and whose appetite for risk would enable us to break new ground. We knew we weren't yet getting noticed by brands that were the household names of today, so we had an idea: Why not link up with those that would be the household names of tomorrow? Why not target fast-growth companies?

On the surface, it appeared to be a good idea: an innovative, aggressive, fast-growing (until recently) advertising agency hooking up with innovative, aggressive, fast-growing clients. It would be fun, it would be in line with our strengths, and it would be a niche all our own.

Step one was to do our homework. We believed that if we could discover some unique marketing challenges that fast-growth companies face, we could find a way to address them and establish our expertise. So we talked to dozens of growth companies. We probed them about what they were doing right, what they were doing wrong, and what kept them up at night. And we learned a great deal.

Not only did we come to understand how fast-growth companies differ from mature companies, we were able to identify four unique growth company profiles. We were so excited by this discovery that we published a report called "The Four Horses."[1] It described the four kinds of growth companies—which we dubbed Thoroughbreds, Fillies, Mules, and Mustangs—and demonstrated how each has unique marketing challenges, opportunities, and needs.

We began to experiment with positioning the agency based on what we had learned. We bought lists of growing companies and sent them direct-mail pieces offering free copies of our study. That generated a few responses, but it didn't get us the bounce we had hoped for. We advertised the report a couple of times in the *Wall*

Street Journal and received a few inquiries, but nothing too promising. We even developed a traveling luncheon presentation to which we could invite growing companies from major markets to present our findings and form new relationships. But after disappointing results, we abandoned that strategy.

It was during one of those trips that the struggles we were having hit home for me, physically, personally, and hard.

I was in the Seattle airport, having just come from a luncheon that can only be described as humiliating. I'd made the trip with Chris Moore, one of our senior account managers. We had rented a lovely hotel banquet room with a beautiful view of Puget Sound. We had worked our invitation list hard and had eighteen confirmed reservations. I had been looking forward to presenting our fascinating research and making several new contacts.

To our surprise and disappointment, out of the eighteen people we expected, just a single CEO showed up. One. It wasn't raining, there weren't any accidents on the freeway, and there was no obvious reason why our confirmed attendees didn't show. They just didn't. We had invested in traveling to Seattle, renting luxury hotel facilities, and buying eighteen expensive lunches for a single prospect who, as it turned out, wasn't a fit for us anyway. It would have been better if no one had come.

It's a little odd making a presentation to one person in a room set up with a podium, a screen, a projector, and tables and chairs for twenty. "Awkward" just doesn't do it justice. Our guest was more than gracious, acting as if nothing was wrong, and suggesting we go ahead with the presentation as planned. Because he took time out of his day to join us, I thought he deserved at least that much. But all I could think of as I made my speech was how badly I wanted to get the humiliation over with and get out of town.

When we left the hotel and made our way to the airport, I thought I would relax and forget about the whole episode. Chris and I had a few minutes before a flight to San Francisco, where we had another luncheon scheduled for the next day. I went to the airport gift shop to find something I could bring home to my kids.

Standing over a table of T-shirts, I saw one I liked and reached across to grab it. As I did, the strap of my briefcase slipped off my shoulder. When I tried to catch it with my forearm, the twenty-pound force yanked me in the opposite direction, wrenching my back. The next thing I knew, I was on my knees.

I was an athlete growing up, and I've experienced my share of injuries. In the past, I had always been able to shake them off. But this one was different. This wasn't a bruise or a pulled muscle: it was (I later found out) a badly herniated disc. The next twenty-four hours were the most excruciating I have ever experienced.

Chris had already gone on to the gate. "If I don't get there," I thought, "he may board the plane and not even miss me until it lands in San Francisco." Alone on the gift shop floor, I picked myself up, forced a smile at the passersby gaping at me, and started painfully making my way toward the gate. It took me about forty-five minutes to make the five-minute walk, but I got there, leaning on the wall, shuffling my feet, and virtually dragging my briefcase behind me. I didn't care what I looked like at that point; all I wanted to do was get on the plane, sit down, and let my back recover.

They say humor equals tragedy plus time, and looking back on my flight, I suppose it was pretty humorous. I happened to have an aisle seat, so I didn't have to climb over other passengers (something I don't think I could have done). But during the short flight from Seattle to San Francisco, both of my seatmates had to go to the bathroom—at different times. That meant I had to stand up and sit down four times as each one came and went. The airplane that I had been looking to as a rest stop instead became a torture chamber. I was hunched over, sweating, and near tears, and all I could think of was getting to my hotel bed where I could convalesce.

By this time, I had the feeling that my injury was pretty serious. When the plane landed, I told Chris that I was badly hurt. He offered to take me to a hospital. But I still thought that all I needed was rest, so he helped me collect my baggage, crawl into a cab, and hobble into the hotel.

We were staying at the Palace, one of San Francisco's magnificent historic properties. It was a stretch for our budget, but we wanted to make a good impression on our luncheon guests. James Korenchen, our public relations director, was waiting for us when we arrived and wasn't expecting to see his boss in such rough shape. After a slow and excruciating walk to my room, I gingerly laid down on the bed and made plans not to move for the next twelve hours. What happened next surprised me.

Instead of relaxing, the muscles in my lower back continued to spasm and tighten, alternating teeth-clenching pain with moments of relief. I thought about calling an ambulance, but I figured all they would do is take me to a hospital where I'd be stuck for days and mess the whole trip up. And I had a luncheon to host tomorrow.

So I stayed on the bed. I didn't eat, I couldn't sleep, and I had no interest in watching TV. All I wanted was for the pain to go away. The lamp by the bed was still on, and it was going to stay on all night. I couldn't bear the thought of reaching to turn it off.

When I awoke after a fitful night's sleep, the pain had begun to subside. But the muscles in my lower back were simply locked. I couldn't stand up straight. I walked down to the lobby like a six-foot man in a hotel full of five-foot ceilings and decided with my team that I was in no shape to make a speech. Chris and James hosted the luncheon while I sat in the lobby. Then they gamely escorted me to the airport.

Standing in line at the ticket counter, I felt like a fool. I didn't really care what the strangers around me thought, but the opinions of my colleagues mattered a great deal. Here I was, their fearless leader, looking like a mere mortal—and a silly one at that. I was embarrassed not only by my hunched-over appearance but by how helpless I felt. I had expected to lead my team to victory and carry home the kill; instead, I was the one being carried home. It was an all-too-appropriate reflection of what I was going through as a leader at the time.

It took weeks for my back to recover and even longer for me to feel good again about my role as the leader of the company. It also took me a while to understand why our strategy wasn't working. Eventually, we realized we had two things working against us.

The first was our own performance. While we had the Inc. 500 award as evidence of our success, it was hard to talk eye to eye with the CEO of a company that was growing by leaps and bounds when our own sales were stagnant. This was probably more a crisis of confidence than anything, but it was the same feeling I had had when surrounded by all the success stories at the Inc. 500 Conference. This problem wasn't insurmountable, but it was uncomfortable.

The second was the deal killer. "The Four Horses" was a great piece of research that reflected real insight into the mistakes growth companies make and the money (either in foregone sales or in marketing inefficiencies) that they leave on the table. But these are not the problems that growing companies are preoccupied with as long as their growth remains strong.

The leaders of the growth companies we were targeting were struggling with things like employee recruitment, facility expansion, and growth financing. They were more concerned with their bankers and lawyers than with their advertising agencies. Marketing simply was not an acute enough pain point to get their attention. While we knew that the practices they were following would likely rise up and bite them one day, it wasn't apparent to them yet. So we couldn't get any traction. Ultimately, we realized we had been pursuing a flawed strategy.

While we were processing all of this, we continued to drift, and the sense in the halls that something was amiss became more palpable every day. But our work was good; the campaigns we developed for our clients were effective, our employees were well treated, and we had a good operation and a good reputation. We just couldn't seem to find the key to getting back on the growth curve.

Fortunately, the story doesn't end there. As the holes in our strategy of serving growth companies became apparent, we couldn't help but notice one of the most interesting findings of our research. Even though every company we had surveyed was prospering, more than one-third of them reported that their marketing efforts were only average or were mediocre.

I wouldn't be surprised at that statistic if the survey had included a broad universe of all companies experiencing varying levels of success. But these were outstanding growth companies, the most successful organizations we could find. Why were they unhappy with their marketing efforts, and more important, what did that mean to their future prospects? There had to be reasons behind that statistic, and we were determined to find out what they were.

One of the advantages of having been named to the Inc. 500 was the exclusive club in which it put us. Despite our current struggles, we had achieved something special and shared a kinship with thousands of other companies that had been recognized since the list was first created in 1982. We came up with the idea of commissioning a second study, this time among not just current growth companies but also those who had achieved lofty heights as much as twenty years earlier. Surely some of them would have struggled since then, and we might be able to learn something from them.

We hired Decision Analyst, a terrific market research firm in Dallas with which we had worked on client projects in the past, to design the study for us. Our goal was to make contact with as many CEOs as we could from companies that had made the Inc. 500 list over the previous twenty years. We designed a comprehensive questionnaire that probed a wide variety of topics surrounding their corporate performance and marketing challenges. And we asked them to rate their companies on a broad battery of metrics that we hoped would shed light on differences in performance.

Out of the several thousand companies that had made the list in the previous twenty years, nearly four hundred answered our questions. While many had continued to achieve rapid growth, 48 percent said they were currently underperforming their sales expectations, and nearly 20 percent had stalled entirely.

What we discovered by studying these companies was fascinating. It gave us a completely new perspective about what really happens when growth stalls and revealed the destructive forces that hinder a struggling company's return to prosperity. That unlocked a new approach to solving our clients' marketing challenges and, not incidentally, helped us come to grips with our own.

Our research gave us new knowledge, to be sure, but it also provided us with something unexpected: empathy. By focusing on other companies that had stalled and trying to help them better understand their problems, we came to better understand our own. Sure, we're marketers, and we're proud of the expertise we bring to the clients we serve. But we're also human and not exempt from the cycles of business.

What we learned is that we weren't ignorant or inept. We were normal. We shouldn't have been surprised that our company would be subject to the same challenges that every company has to face at some point in its existence. We simply didn't know about them. The most encouraging thing we learned is that the normal course of business events got us into this situation, and we believed we could take the steps necessary to get us out.

Fortunately, by applying what we've learned, we've regained our footing. We were able to avoid layoffs during our struggle, brought on board Bart Cleveland, a nationally respected creative director, and step-by-step returned to the growth curve. We've averaged just over 20 percent annual revenue growth for the past four years—enough to keep us moving forward and enhancing our capabilities, but not so much that we can't keep quality high as we adjust to our new size. We certainly don't take growth for granted this time around, especially as global financial and economic problems have wiped out millions of jobs and trillions of dollars of wealth. But we do feel better equipped to deal with the challenges we're facing.

Since we first embarked on this phase of our journey, I've spoken with many leaders of struggling companies. They're not stupid people. They are bright, articulate, intelligent professionals who simply ran into a set of unfamiliar circumstances that, like ours, caused their companies' growth to stall. That's all.

So if your company is struggling at the moment, take heart. You may feel as if you're failing, but you may be as much the victim as the cause of your company's problems. And understanding the whys behind your woes, which this book will help you do, is the first step to fixing them.

On the other hand, if your company is still doing well, it's good that you're reading this now. The simple truth is that growth is never guaranteed. Practically every organization will face a growth decline at some point in its history. You may be able to minimize or even avoid altogether a slump by understanding and applying the principles put forth here.

When Growth Stalls isn't just another book of business advice by a consultant, professor, or MBA who has studied a subject from afar. It's a book about lessons learned the hard way, brought to you by someone who has faced the same problems you may be facing today. I survived to tell about them, and as you apply these lessons, I'm confident you will, too.

2

Growth Stalls

From the vantage point I now have about the ups and downs of business cycles (and the inevitability of stalled growth), my investing strategies of the late 1990s now seem like—to borrow the term famously popularized by Alan Greenspan—irrational exuberance. But during that time I, like millions of other investors, could do no wrong. I'll never forget attending "The Champions Institute," a special retreat in Snowmass, Colorado, for high performers in the advertising industry, where my boss at the time had sent me as a reward for my hard work.

The speakers were amazing. They included Lee Garfinkel of Lowe & Partners, crowned "America's Best Creative Director" by *Adweek* magazine; Bob Herbold, chief operating officer of Microsoft, who shared the fascinating story behind the release of Windows 95; and a gentleman I had never heard of named Ted Leonsis, who ran a fairly new company called America Online. All of the speakers were terrific, but Leonsis made the greatest impact on me. I remember him smiling, so sure of himself, as he explained AOL's business model to a roomful of Internet neophytes.

Leonsis got me excited about the developing Internet economy, and when I got home, I set up an account with Charles Schwab & Co. and began to experience the joy of online trading. I bought Sun Microsystems, makers of high-end servers that were selling well to the financial services and telecommunications industries. I bought Intel, the company behind the microprocessors that were driving the new economy. I bought Cisco, too; at the time, I wasn't sure what a router did, but I knew it had something to do with the Internet, and that had to be good. As my money grew, I also bought Earthlink, WebMD, Sprint PCS, Dell, Nokia, Adobe, and Level 3 Communications. I even bought stock in a crazy start-up that spun out of Sandia National Laboratories called Muse Technologies, whose data-modeling technology was so advanced, so innovative—and so cool—it couldn't go wrong.

You know what happened. After several years of convincing myself I had the Midas touch, I realized I wasn't so smart after all. The tech bubble burst, and like millions of other investors, I got good and wet. Fortunately, I didn't have my life savings wrapped up in these companies. But I learned two valuable lessons: number one, insane market momentum can't go on forever; and number two, even in the best-run companies, growth stalls. That's a truth I've come to understand much better in the years I've been studying growth dynamics.

Consider one of the most popular and influential business books of our generation: *Built to Last* by Jim Collins and Jerry Porras. Based on solid research, the book highlights eighteen visionary companies that managed to stay atop the business world through the ups and downs of four turbulent decades (1950–1990). In the book, the authors themselves noted that "as extraordinary as they are, the visionary companies do not have perfect, unblemished records."[1] Indeed, since *Built to Last* was published in 1994, more than half of these "truly exceptional" companies have suffered from one or more years of revenue declines.

At some point in almost every company's history, growth stalls. It doesn't matter how well the organization is managed, how great its products are, or how appealing its marketing and advertising are. Growth stalls in every industry, it stalls in every phase of the economic cycle, and it stalls no matter who gets elected president of the United States.

Generating consistent growth is just plain hard, no matter how smart, experienced, or talented you are. As one of the company leaders we interviewed told us, it's like "trying to keep an ice cube from melting." It can be done, but only in the right environment.

Understanding that environment is what the research we embarked on was all about. Following our initial study in 2003, we spent the next five years interviewing companies, reviewing the literature, and testing our findings in the marketplace. Then in 2008 we went back out again for a second round of interviews. We started with 5,696 companies in all fifty states. We didn't limit ourselves to former high flyers; we wanted to get a cross-section of all companies across America. More than half served consumer markets, with about a third of them business-to-business and the rest government contractors.

Although the study was conducted at a different time, in a different economy, with a different respondent profile than our original research, the results were remarkably consistent. Nearly 14 percent of companies in the study were currently stalled, and more than

**Figure 2.1. Companies Stalled in Past Decade (41.2%)
and Those Currently Stalled (13.7%)
Versus All Companies Studied.**

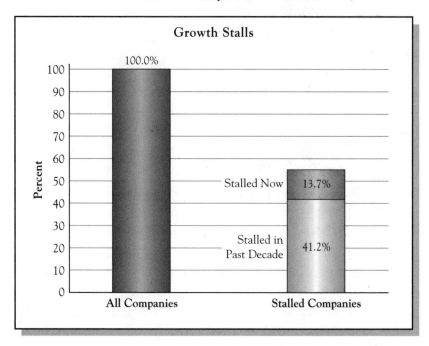

40 percent of those that remained reported that their growth had stalled within the last one to ten years. That means that in the past decade, more than half of all companies we surveyed have experienced a stall. That's a big group.

We then zeroed in on a subset of companies that were struggling and compared them with a random sample of overall respondents. Our goal was to isolate stalled companies not from high-growth performers but from average corporations. We found that there was no way to hide from growth challenges. Business-to-business companies were just as likely to have stalled as consumer companies, and not even government contractors were safe.

Size doesn't matter either. Of the companies we looked at closely, 36 percent were under $30 million in revenue, 31 percent were between $31 million and $250 million, and 33 percent were over $250 million. We found no statistically significant differences in stall rates between the biggest and smallest companies.

Our subject companies had achieved a wide range of market share as well: from less than 1 percent to more than 50 percent. The only significant variation we found in propensity to stall was that those who were market share leaders were better able to maintain growth. Those ranked number two and below in their markets were all equally likely to have struggled. The problem was particularly acute for weaker industry players: those companies whose market share was so small they didn't even know where they ranked were twice as likely to have stalled.

It may not be surprising to know that stalled companies are more likely to have higher turnover, lower margins, weaker customer loyalty, and tougher cash flow issues than companies experiencing healthy growth. But we were most struck in our research by the high correlation between stalled revenue growth and unhealthy internal dynamics: issues involving trust and respect, the inability to make lasting decisions, a paralyzing lack of confidence, a tendency to overthink things, and in a strange dichotomy, a propensity to either resist change or switch directions too frequently. The remarkable thing about these factors is that they're all internal, psychological in nature, and highly destructive. And they do a lot of damage simply by going unrecognized.

As you think about your own company, you may or may not immediately recognize some of these factors. Keep in mind, however, that these internal dynamics are like pepper in your teeth: just because you don't see them doesn't mean they're not there. Over the course of five years, two major studies, and a host of consulting projects, we have seen that the probability of a struggling company suffering from some or even most of these factors is quite high.

No Company Is Safe

Who would have thought that once-venerable companies like Bear Stearns, Lehman Brothers, and Merrill Lynch could be bankrupt or sold at fire-sale prices virtually overnight? That after years of robust economic growth, the stock market could experience its worst week ever—worse than even any single week during the Great Depression? And that excesses in one sector (mortgage lending) could lead to wide-ranging damage across the global economy?

In today's globalized world, every company is interconnected, and seemingly unrelated events cause a destructive ripple effect throughout the larger system. As the astonishing events of the 2008 credit crunch continue to unfold, we can learn lessons from previous downturns.

When the tech bubble burst in 2000, it wasn't just dot-coms that went in the tank. In 2001 McDonald's, America's leading hamburger joint (and a traditional bricks-and-mortar business if there ever was one), saw same-store sales—the critical metric in the fast-food industry—decline by 1.3 percent. The following year was worse: a decline of more than 2 percent. Then in 2003 the company made a turnaround credited to a variety of things, from introducing a popular line of salads to slowing the growth of new restaurants. It then went on a five-year run of same-store sales gains until 2008, when revenues again went flat.

Unlike many companies, McDonald's has been through such cycles before and understands that growth stalls. Jim Skinner, CEO, says, "While we generate better results in a booming economy, like everyone else, we've navigated through tough times before, and we're confident we can do it again."[2]

There are plenty of other examples. IBM went from making $6 billion to losing $8 billion in just three short years, and it took four years to get earnings back up again.[3] Janus Funds went from Wall Street's penthouse to its doghouse almost overnight during the dot-com bust. Even Dell, which grew from a dorm-room start-up to the world's largest computer maker in less than two decades, has learned some hard lessons. Company spokesman T. R. Reid proudly proclaimed in 2001, "We built our organization for a market growth at 15% to 18% [annually]."[4] Fast-forward five years to the fourth quarter of 2006, when Dell's worldwide PC sales declined 8.7 percent.[5] Semiretired Michael Dell had to step back in to rescue his struggling company and was a little more contrite: "The direct model has been a revolution but is not a religion," he said. "The old model ran its course; now it's time for a new course."[6]

And then there's Home Depot, a behemoth with more than 2,200 stores and 350,000 employees. Home Depot grew to $50 billion in revenue faster than any other retailer in history, and today it has grown well past that benchmark. For the first twenty-five years of its existence, it was the darling of growth companies. It is one of the greatest business success stories of our time, but even Home Depot is not immune to stalled growth. From 2005 to 2006, Home Depot's same-store sales went from an increase of 3.8 percent to a 2.8 percent decline—a painful 6.6 percentage point swing. In 2008 the company reported its first full-year loss in history and a 2.1 percent revenue decline to $77.3 billion.[7] Same-store sales in the summer of 2008 tumbled an incredible 7.9 percent (despite the issuance of some 100 million tax rebate checks by the U.S. Internal Revenue Service).[8] No wonder chief marketing officer Roger Adams declared in an interview with *Advertising Age*, "We need to start all over."[9]

Like most companies we studied, Home Depot's problems stem from a variety of factors. They have had to face increasingly aggressive competition, particularly from their closest rival, Lowe's. They've been forced to cope with a poor housing market due to the mortgage meltdown, which reduces the resources available to homeowners for investing in renovations. And the dynamics of their business are changing as well: good locations for massive 130,000-square-foot warehouses are getting harder to find. But while these issues may hit Home Depot, as the market leader, particularly hard, they affect its competitors as well. External factors alone do not account for all of the company's problems.

One longtime Home Depot management employee I spoke with had a front-row seat to the dismantling of the company's famous customer-first culture under the management team headed by Bob Nardelli. He watched as the newly centralized inventory management system resulted in out-of-stock items and made local inventory customization nearly impossible ("You have to live with what we send you," he was told by corporate headquarters). He cringed as he watched long-established incentives and bonus plans get dismantled. Most significantly, he mourned the loss of a spirit in which customer service came first, quoting one former customer who said, "You'd have an easier time finding Bin Laden than an associate at Home Depot."[10]

The manager I spoke to is not a disgruntled former employee. He still works within the company and clearly loves it. He just hates seeing what happened to it.

He described the new leadership as unintentionally "building mediocrity into the system": losing the best people, promoting "C" performers, hiring on the cheap, and implementing crazy, paper-pushing policies. "We laughed at Lowe's when they put in 'Help' buttons," he told me. "We thought it was a joke—we're Home Depot, we have people on the floor, we don't need buttons." But where there used to be thirteen to fifteen people working in a typical Home Depot department, now they were down to two or three, making Help buttons appear a logical solution—or an unfortunate necessity.

"Sure, we may have been a little extravagant in how many associates we had on the floor," he said, "and there's nothing wrong with a little streamlining. But this was almost like how the government acts after a flood: instead of helping people in the field, they set up a chain-link fence. And there was nobody in corporate you could talk to; that's just the way it was."

He told me that in the old days, seven or eight people would compete for new management openings, but in recent years it has been hard to give the positions away. He heard managers joking that one undeserving but recently promoted employee came from the "No Associate Left Behind" program. "You go to a staff meeting and just shake your head," he said. "It's so backwards. They're so caught up in chasing paperwork."

As disillusionment filtered throughout the management ranks, he says, many of Home Depot's best employees began to ask "what if" questions about their own futures. The company's lost focus caused many of its managers to take their own eyes off the ball. At the critical CMO position, Home Depot had five different people in a seven-year stretch.[11]

So what, exactly, went wrong at Home Depot? Sure, the company had to deal with external challenges to growth such as a difficult economic environment and aggressive competition, but every company has to deal with those. And it's not as if the board brought in a novice in Nardelli; he was a smart, accomplished senior executive from one of the most celebrated companies in business, General Electric. I believe what really hurt Home Depot is a damaging shift in powerful internal dynamics that nobody saw coming.

There was a strong business case for the changes that Nardelli and his team implemented; they made financial sense and were hard to argue with. But the management team had no way of foreseeing the damaging internal effect those changes would have, upsetting the cultural equilibrium that had so successfully served Home Depot since its founding. The powerful role internal dynamics such as these play in causing stalled growth—and the crippling effects they have on companies trying to return to the growth curve—is the basis of this book.

While Home Depot's specific issues are unique to the company, they fit a pattern that we see in other stalled companies we've studied. From corporate behemoths like Sprint, Sears, and Circuit City to midsized players like Einstein Bros. Bagels and Zippo Lighters, to small companies like Muni Financial and M² Consulting, certain patterns repeat themselves.

Bain & Company did a study of what drives profitable growth over time and found that only one in seven companies achieves reasonable growth for five straight years, even though every company says it wants to grow and takes great pains to do so.

As striking as that statistic sounds, it rings true. And there is a great deal of information in the secondary literature about why this is the case. In its own study of growth companies, Deloitte & Touche (now Deloitte) suggested that young companies in particular are susceptible to stalling because they don't have the "growth infrastructure" to maintain continual revenue increases.[12] Scientists at the Woodside Institute, a research organization focused on innovation, take a more academic perspective and cite a host of factors that cause growth to stall, including "technological discontinuities, regulatory upheavals, geopolitical shocks, industry deverticalization and disintermediation, abrupt shifts in consumer tastes, and hordes of nontraditional competitors."[13]

There may be truth in all of these observations. But as an executive myself, I tend to favor the simple framework presented by Philip M. Rosenzweig, author of "The Halo Effect": "The business world is not a place of clear causal relationships, where a given set of actions leads to predictable results, but one that is more tenuous and uncertain. The simple fact is that no formula can guarantee a company's success, at least not in a competitive business environment."[14]

One of the corporate leaders we interviewed likened the challenge of generating consistent growth to that of creating a perpetual motion machine. We know from physics that such a machine can not exist. But we also know that an object in motion can maintain its momentum for a long, long time when acted on by an external force (the earth has been in orbit around the sun since time began). What we've learned is that by understanding and applying the principles of internal psychological health that we uncovered in our research, you can be that force on behalf of your company. If your organization is going to prosper (or possibly even survive) long term, you'll need to be.

Ries Robinson, chairman and CEO of InLight Solutions, said something to me at lunch one day during my struggle with stalled growth that has stuck with me ever since: "An entrepreneur is someone who can make progress in an ambiguous environment." There's no more ambiguous environment than the one within a company experiencing stalled growth.

Progress is still possible, but acceptance must come first. There will always be obstacles to growth in your company's path; that's the painful fact. But if you understand those obstacles—and the damaging chain of events they can set in motion—they can be overcome.

3

Market Tectonics

On the morning of May 12, 2008, the sun rose over the Sichuan Province of China just as it had every other day. Parents roused their children out of bed and sent them off to school, then headed off to the factories and fields for another long day of work. But at 2:28 PM local time, the familiar buzz of the busy province was interrupted by the horrific sounds of buildings shaking and glass breaking as an earthquake measuring 7.9 on the Richter scale rolled through the region. Tens of thousands of people lost their lives, and millions were left homeless.

Scientists later explained what had happened. According to the U.S. Geological Survey, the earthquake resulted from "the convergence of crustal material slowly moving from the high Tibetan Plateau, to the west, against strong crust underlying the Sichuan Basin and southeastern China."[1] When landforms that large move, something has to give, causing the earth to quake, foundations to shake, and buildings to crumble. While some structures in Sichuan Province held up better than others, nothing in central China was exempt from the quake's effects, as it was felt as far away as Shanghai, 1,700 kilometers to the east. That's the way it is when continental shelves shift, a principle scientists call plate tectonics.

There are similar principles at work in the world of commerce. I call them "market tectonics" because, like plate tectonics, they're unavoidable facts of life driven by forces far greater and more powerful than any individual or organization can control. While market tectonics are not nearly as serious or as deadly as plate tectonics, they share similar characteristics in that they affect every company, often come as a surprise, and can cause a great deal of damage to those who aren't prepared to deal with them. Just ask AIG, which was caught completely unprepared by the unraveling of the financial markets that began when the real estate bubble burst and ended up in a pile of rubble.

Although each stalled company's story is unique, our research has found that when growth stalls, market tectonics almost always play a role, with the specific forces tending to fall into certain predictable categories. Economic upheavals, aggressive competition, and changing industry dynamics are challenges that every company eventually faces, regardless of its age, industry, or track record. As inevitable as these external forces are, however, they often catch company leaders flat-footed and ill prepared.

Before you can determine what to do when growth stalls, it helps to have some perspective on why it happens.

Economic Factors

By the end of 2001, my investment in Sun Microsystems wasn't looking so smart. The company was suffering the effects of the slowdown (two of their biggest customers would soon be filing for bankruptcy), and companies were unloading used Sun servers on the grey market, further depressing demand. Then Sun took a huge hit in September, a month that usually accounts for nearly half their annual sales, as the events of September 11 stopped buyers in their tracks. Shortly thereafter, Sun reported its first quarterly loss in a dozen years, laid off nearly four thousand employees, and shuttered facilities.[2] Having announced multiple rounds of layoffs in 2008, the company still is not out of the woods.[3]

Sun's story is not unique. In fact, the leading cause of revenue problems among the stalled companies we studied was related to economic factors. Business leaders know that the economy is cyclical, but none of us know when the cycles of expansion and contraction are going to hit. Sun was a well-run corporation with a good suite of products that was simply hit hard by economic woes caused by the tech bust. But Sun's problems pale in comparison with those of other notable companies.

When Lucent Technologies was spun off from AT&T, it seemed like a can't-lose proposition. The company occupied a sweet spot within the new economy, manufacturing a variety of products for the telecommunications industry. Once it left its former parent's nest, Lucent became an attractive vendor to AT&T competitors it couldn't previously serve. And the company lived up to its early billings, generating some $40 billion in revenue, employing 151,000 people, and boasting a market capitalization of a quarter of a trillion dollars. Its stock traded as high as $84 per share.

But in just four short years, Lucent's revenue had fallen by 75 percent, more than one hundred thousand of its employees were gone, and it had lost 95 percent of its market capitalization. The company's stock price dropped to as low at 55 cents. The bursting of the dot-com bubble had shut down Lucent's fountain of growth, a problem magnified by the heavy discounts and risky financing terms Lucent had been providing its customers to meet aggressive sales targets. The company was so highly leveraged that when the recession hit, it had nowhere to turn.[4] Reflecting on that difficult time, Chief Financial Officer Frank D'Amello said, "We went from what was the perfect market to the perfect storm."[5]

In 2002 Lucent was the worst five-year performer in the *Wall Street Journal*'s annual Shareholder Scorecard.[6] Four years later, it merged with Alcatel, and Lucent's brief, ten-year run as an independent company came to an inauspicious end.

Sun Microsystems and Lucent Technologies were unfortunate victims of an ill-timed economic crunch. But technology companies weren't the only ones hamstrung by the dot-com bust. In 2002, the same year that Lucent topped the list of the *Wall Street Journal*'s worst five-year performers, a women's clothing retailer called Chico's was at the top of the best five-year performers list. Chico's generated over a half-billion dollars in annual revenue, was opening fifty new stores a year, and had achieved same-store sales gains for nineteen of the previous twenty quarters. But by 2008—in the middle of another economic downturn—Chico's same-store sales had declined by more than 20 percent.[7]

Other retailers found themselves in the same boat. Nordstrom, Kohl's, JC Penney, Gap, American Eagle, Banana Republic, Ann Taylor, Zales, and many other leading retailers reported same-store sales declines in 2008 (Walmart fared better, in part because of its low-price appeal).[8]

D. R. Horton, the nation's largest home builder, struggled mightily as a result of the subprime mortgage mess. In the third quarter of 2008, new home closings fell 36 percent, cancellations hit 39 percent, and the company suffered an overall revenue decline of 44 percent over the previous year.[9] KB Home, one of D. R. Horton's biggest competitors, fared even worse, with a 75 percent decrease in new home orders and a 53 percent cancellation rate in early 2008.[10]

Thornburg Mortgage got caught in the undertow as well. Thornburg created a niche by providing highly secure adjustable-rate jumbo mortgages to only the most credit-worthy borrowers. Despite the fact that Thornburg had a much lower-than-average delinquency rate and never dealt in subprime mortgages, the company faced nearly $2 billion in margin calls from its biggest creditors that risked bankrupting it. When Thornburg shares fell an incredible 86 percent in one week, CEO Larry Goldstone protested, "Quite simply, the panic that has gripped the mortgage-financing market is irrational and has no basis in investment reality."[11]

Thornburg, like D. R. Horton and KB Home, got caught in what economists call a "margin spiral," where problems in one sector of the economy rapidly ripple across other sectors, often irrationally. At one point in 2008, nearly 10 percent of the 9,194 companies tracked by Standard & Poor's Compustat research service had market capitalizations that were *lower* than their cash holdings.[12] As with plate tectonics, not being at the epicenter doesn't shield you from the quake's effects. When the economy craters, there's nowhere to hide.

But what about so-called recession-proof industries? Aren't some companies providing services so vital that they thrive even in hard times? There's certainly no dearth of such claims. But Cynthia Crossen, a *Wall Street Journal* columnist, offers a cautionary historical perspective on them: "Since the 1930s, claims to immunity from economic downturns have become popular marketing tools. Only the industries that claim invulnerability have changed. In recent decades, businesses insisting that they were recession-proof include weddings and honeymoons, pipe organs, Oriental rugs, Jaguars, auto parts, Tupperware, Ultralight airplanes, bubble gum, Hershey's chocolate, chocolate truffles, Italian restaurants, Burger King, household plants, fitness centers, skiing, guns, power tools, gospel music, prisons, minivans, and many more."[13]

Crossen goes on to quote Robert Whaples, professor of economics at Wake Forest University: "There's nothing that could be called recession-proof," he says. "There are just degrees of recession-proof."[14]

That's even true for the venture capital industry (those entrepreneurial kingpins who invest millions of investor dollars in unproven ventures and, in most years, rake in more). The industry as a whole experienced three consecutive years of negative returns from 2001 to 2004, and returns since have been tepid.[14] Nobody escapes the economic cycle.

Fortunately, there are things companies can do to protect themselves from the worst effects of an economic downturn. Some ideas apply to every sector of the economy and have been proved through cycle after cycle of growth and contraction.

To ride out a downturn, it's important for every company to "store nuts." That's the advice an entrepreneur friend gave me when we launched our firm. Having been in business for decades, he had witnessed the effects of economic contractions and knew that having money in the bank was not just smart, it was strategic. Having lived through two recessions as a corporate leader myself, I've benefited from the wisdom of his counsel. During good times, build up a cash reserve and avoid the temptation to spend like there's no tomorrow. There is a tomorrow, and it may be a rainy day.

Another principle: Prudence beats panic. While you may need to trim your expenses, don't cut any deeper than you have to. When Circuit City ran into rough waters in 2007, the company laid off

3,400 employees, saving $200 million in expenses. But they replaced many of those employees with lower-paid, less-experienced staff and lost nearly $500 million in gross profit as frustrated customers shopped elsewhere.[15] You can cut your way to survival but not to success.

It's also important, even in hard times, to maintain or (if possible) increase strategic investments. During the Great Depression, Procter & Gamble continued to launch new products (Dreft detergent) and pioneer new marketing strategies (sponsoring radio serials and soap operas). More recently, during the recession of 2001, the company launched both Crest Whitestrips and Swiffer WetJet,[16] and in 2008 it began testing a dry cleaning service, a once-a-week toothpaste, and a new line of products that freshen up clothes without washing.[17] Just as smart investors know the time to buy is when everybody else is selling, smart companies know that downturns will lead to upturns, and the better the use they've made of their marketing and research and development budgets, the bigger the jump they'll get on their competition when things pick up again.

The most important thing to remember when hard times hit is to keep your wits about you. Protect your assets, play for the long term, and make sure your people know you have a plan.

Aggressive Competition

In our first study, which focused exclusively on fast-growth companies, nearly 60 percent said they had been pioneers in their niche. That means that at one point they had 100 percent market share. But by the time we interviewed them, they were at various stages of their life cycles and reported an average market share of just 16 percent. These companies, like virtually all companies, had been hit by another hard reality of business—aggressive competition. According to our research, it's the second most common reason for growth stalling.

Competition has always been a fact of business life, but today it's more aggressive than ever. In this era of rapid commoditization, fewer and fewer companies can maintain long-standing differentiation that insulates them from competitive encroachment. Think about the brands all around you. Can you really tell the difference between Applebee's and Chili's? Between OfficeMax and Office Depot? Between Ford and Chevy? Most consumers have their favorites, but competition provides plenty of acceptable substitutes. I heard the story of a flight attendant who was asked if she ever tired of saying "good-bye" over and over as passengers exit the plane. "No," she said, "What I get really tired of is saying 'Is Pepsi OK?'" Unfortunately for Coke, for most people Pepsi is just fine.

Lucent's merger with Alcatel didn't end its problems. The marriage was intended, among other things, to allow the combined company to cut unnecessary costs and maintain margins. But shortly after the merger, the company's biggest rival, Ericsson, launched "Project Stealth," an initiative to achieve 40 percent worldwide wireless market share. Speaking of his new competitor, Bert Norberg, Ericsson's executive vice president of sales and marketing, said, "We knew their management would be distracted and preoccupied."[18]

Alcatel-Lucent had to plow any savings it realized into lowering prices in an effort to fend off the competitive threat. Ten months after the merger, the company had lost $12 billion in market capitalization, about the value of Lucent alone before the deal. You could almost see former CEO Patricia Russo shaking her head as she said, "It's basically as if we have the worst of all worlds in year one."[19]

Aggressive competition is found in every industry—high tech and low, business-to-business and business-to-consumer, new and old. RadioShack is an American institution, but it hasn't been able to match the aggressive expansion and pricing power of category leader Best Buy, and it has closed more than five hundred stores, shuttered five service centers, and laid off fifteen hundred employees.[20]

Kmart filed for Chapter 11 bankruptcy in January 2002, the largest retailer ever to do so. The company boarded up 13 percent of its locations and cut twenty-two thousand jobs.[21] Why? Two words: Target and Walmart.

Kleenex is another iconic brand. It has been around since 1924, and its name is synonymous with its best-known product. But Kleenex has to fight not only behemoth Procter & Gamble, with its Puff's Plus line of tissues, but also generic brands, niche players like

Olay, and even Starbucks. Why Starbucks? Because now that coffee shops and fast-food restaurants are daily stops for millions of Americans, instead of reaching for a Kleenex, many people grab that spare napkin they picked up with their burger or java. Each of these competitors has taken a bite out of Kleenex's franchise, and sales were down 9.7 percent in 2006. Steve Erb, the company's associate marketing director, even blames advances in cold medicine for declines in Kleenex usage. "Over-the-counter and prescribed medicines are much better at treating the symptoms," he says.[22]

And then there's Dell. As recently as February 2005, the *Wall Street Journal* reported that solid third-quarter results "solidify Dell's increasingly rock-steady lead in the personal-computer market as some competitors wobble." Kevin Rollins, Dell's then-CEO, referred to the quarter as "the best operating period in Dell's history."[23] That same week, Mark Hurd replaced Carly Fiorina at Dell's ailing rival Hewlett-Packard.

Bill Coleman, CEO of BEA Systems, captured the mystique of the post-dot-com-era Dell when he said, "If the motivating fear of big companies over the past five years was 'getting Amazoned,' the real danger going forward is 'getting Delled.'"[24]

But as it turned out, Dell is the one that got Delled. As its long-standing cost advantages were largely duplicated by competitors, Dell's PC sales began to shrink, declining by nearly 9 percent by the end of 2006 while a resurgent HP's grew by more than 23 percent. Hurd was hailed as a hero, and Rollins met an ignominious end.[25]

Our research shows that, generally speaking, the healthiest companies are those whose industry barriers to entry are high, whose differentiation is growing, or ideally, both. In rapidly maturing industries (like PC manufacturing), it's hard to maintain either.

When barriers to entry are low, numerous companies jump into the marketplace. In time, the market offers many acceptable alternatives to a particular product or service, and perceived value declines, negatively impacting both revenue and profitability.

Shortly after the introduction of the videocassette recorder, the video-rental market began to take off. For the first time, consumers could rent movies and enjoy them in the privacy of their own homes whenever they wanted. No longer were they at the mercy of Hollywood or the television networks in determining what and when they could watch. The retail video-rental market had low barriers to entry: all someone needed to get into the business was space at a strip mall and the money to purchase a small inventory of videocassettes. As a result, mom-and-pop video stores sprang up on almost every corner overnight.

Blockbuster quickly became the dominant video-rental chain by raising barriers to entry. By creating a strong brand and acquiring (or forcing out of business) smaller, undercapitalized operators, Blockbuster became the most familiar, most convenient, and most dependable video retailer. The company's scale enabled it not only to go public (generating additional capital it used to fuel growth), but also to negotiate a groundbreaking revenue-sharing agreement with the major movie studios, further enhancing its competitive advantage. Blockbuster became the most successful player in its category simply by following a strategy to raise its industry's barriers to entry. (As I write, Blockbuster is struggling, a victim of changing dynamics. Read on.)

Differentiation can be another important bulwark against competition. Because it creates scarcity, differentiation enhances perceived value and improves margins. When competitors are able to duplicate your offerings, differentiation fades, and your ability to charge a price premium declines (or vanishes altogether). But even in the most competitive, commoditized industries, differentiation is possible.

Take diamonds, for example. Two diamonds that share the same "four Cs" (color, cut, clarity, and carat weight) are indistinguishable from one another and identical in value. Yet, the same diamond you could pick up at, say, Zales would sell for significantly more at Tiffany. Through the use of imaginative and consistent branding (from store location to customer service to that famous blue box), Tiffany has carved out a niche for which customers are willing to pay a hefty premium.

It's a rare company that remains sheltered from competition for long. And competition is not only unavoidable, it's uncontrollable.

There comes a point in the life cycle of many companies when they hit what we call the First Wall.

It's a classic story: An organization pioneers a new product, a new service, or a new way of doing business. The company grows fast and enjoys healthy margins. But inevitably, its success attracts competitors. Differentiation gets hazier. Margins suffer. Growth stalls. This is the First Wall syndrome.

There are many examples of companies hitting the First Wall, some of them fatal. Netscape hit it hard and fast when Microsoft launched Internet Explorer. Google quickly caught and passed its industry sibling Yahoo!. And Pottery Barn, which defined a whole new category of home decorating retailer, saw its five-year run of 22 percent average earnings growth slow to a trickle in 2007 as copycats from Restoration Hardware to Target went after its niche. Williams-Sonoma, parent company of Pottery Barn, even sued Target for allegedly copying its designs.[26] That's what happens when your customers spend nearly three times as much on home decorating as the average consumer. Success breeds imitation.

Palm did not invent the personal digital assistant (Apple's Newton would get the credit for that), but with the Treo they did devise the first successful "smart phone." The phones were so popular that external developers designed some thirty thousand applications for them.[27] But with the market growing at a double-digit pace, Palm was bound to attract competitors, and it did. Handspring, founded by the developers of the original Palm Pilot, came out with a product featuring virtually identical capabilities (my first "Palm," in fact, was a Handspring). Motorola and Nokia did the same. Alternate platforms like the BlackBerry and Apple's iPhone chipped away at Palm's market share, the latter outselling Treos by a two-to-one margin shortly after its introduction. Despite double-digit gains in overall smart-phone sales in recent years, Palm's sales have declined, and its smart-phone market share now lags that of both BlackBerry and Apple.[28]

Companies that have enjoyed long-term success understand that as markets mature, differences blur. They know that their challenge is not necessarily to be better than the competition but to stay different.

Whether a company is young or old, public or private, the challenges of competition stay the same. The more success you attain, the more quickly and aggressively competitors will invade your turf. You have to stay one step ahead of them, and it's a struggle that never ends.

As with economic challenges, there are proven strategies companies can use to lessen the impact aggressive competitors have on their market share. There isn't space here to describe these competitive strategies in detail—whole books have been written on the subject—but there are some basics that every company should keep in mind as it faces competitors who want what it's got.

Keep close tabs on your competition. Our research shows that it's not always necessary to outspend your competitors, but it is necessary to outthink them. The struggling companies we studied were less likely to keep good tabs on their competitors' efforts and, as a result, were more likely to be caught off guard by new products, new services, or new strategies they launched.

Consistently look for ways to enhance and protect your differentiation. There's no such thing as a static market, and if you're

Figure 3.1. Companies That Somewhat or Strongly Agree That "Our Competitive Differentiation Is Growing" (Stalled, 33%; Healthy, 64%).

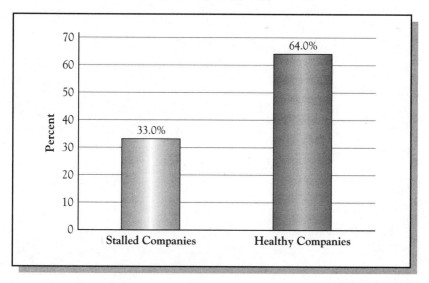

winning today, there are bound to be competitors on your tail. Companies in our research that reported growing differentiation were more likely to report healthy revenue growth than those that did not.

Look to enhance strategic partnerships with other players in your value chain. They face competitive pressures as well, and a changing marketplace may increase their willingness to do business differently. Perhaps they will extend you better terms or more exclusivity in exchange for a long-term commitment, or they will partner with you on a speculative basis to develop new initiatives.

Invest aggressively in research and development, always looking for both incremental improvements and major breakthroughs that will make the products and services you offer increasingly difficult to beat. Competitive markets are breeding grounds for innovation. If you're not the innovator, you're likely to be a victim of one.

Changing Industry Dynamics

Economic peaks and troughs are predictable; you may not know when they're going to hit, but you know they're coming and you can take preventive measures to deal with them. Competition is predictable as well. Again, it may not be clear when and from where it's coming, but companies can take steps to keep their organizations on solid competitive footing.

But the world never stops turning, and while some market tectonics are predictable (Pfizer's patents on its $13 billion cholesterol drug Lipitor will begin to expire in 2010), others come as a surprise.[29] We call these *changing industry dynamics*, and they are yet another significant reason why growth stalls. In fact, struggling companies we studied were more than three times more likely than others to say that the marketplace had changed and they no longer knew their place in it.

The most notable example of changing dynamics in our generation is the Internet, which has spawned entirely new business models and whole new industries. When I overheard my friends

Figure 3.2. Companies That Somewhat or Strongly Agree That "The Marketplace Has Changed and We Don't Know Our Place in It" (Stalled, 29%; Healthy, 8.5%).

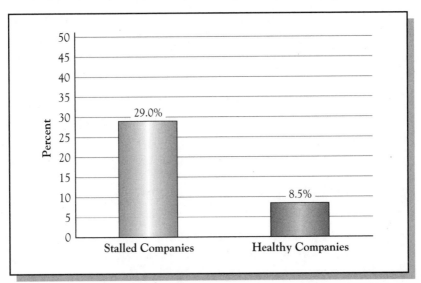

who work in engineering talk about "the Internet" in the early 1990s, I thought they were referring to their companies' internal e-mail systems. I had no idea how radically that odd new word would change my business—and life in general—in the coming years.

Many other types of changing industry dynamics can have crippling effects on companies, from technological advances (broadband, the rise of satellite radio) to demographic shifts (the aging of the baby boomers) to government policy changes (the federal bailout of the financial system, cap-and-trade legislation). Just think about how the retail business has changed in our lifetime. Woolworth used to be a household name, but changing dynamics have at various times favored department stores like Sears and JC Penney, specialty retailers like Gap and Limited, and now discounters like Walmart and Target.

Remember when Microsoft was untouchable, and its monopolistic hold on the software industry put it squarely in the government's antitrust sights? How rapidly times have changed: Microsoft is still rich and powerful, but with the ascent of Google, it looks positively vulnerable.

Similarly, the problems facing midscale restaurants aren't only related to the economy. For fifty years more women entered the workforce every year. The trend took away their time to cook but filled their pocketbooks with a second income, and both factors were a boon to the restaurant industry. But that trend has leveled off, and the percentage of women in the workforce has actually now slightly declined. That changing dynamic makes competition even fiercer as industry players fight for the same slice of a shrinking pie.[30]

Consider these trends and the impact they've had on companies:

- Web-based and video-on-demand services, eroding the dominance of once-unassailable Blockbuster

- Health and nutrition trends, which have led to declines in the carbonated soft drink industry as sales of specialty waters, sports drinks, and coffee each drain away their share

- Advances in telecommunications, as mobile phones and VOIP (Voice Over Internet Protocol) change consumer habits. Qwest alone lost more than a million customers in 2007 and shortly thereafter announced layoffs due to the decline in landline phone service[31]

- Specialty hospitals carving out the most profitable health care niches (heart care, orthopedics, cosmetic surgery), squeezing the profitability of general community hospitals that have to care for the sickest patients, no matter their condition or disease

- iPods and other MP3 players, wreaking havoc on the traditional music distribution system

Getty Images rose to prominence in the stock film-and-footage industry through a combination of good service, strategic acquisitions, and smart distribution agreements that gave it the rights to photo collections of companies such as Time Life and National Geographic. (Getty generates more than half its revenue from companies like mine, as we license images for use in ads, on brochures, and in Web sites.) But the combination of digital imaging, easy uploading, and the giant universal catalogue called the Internet has created a vast secondary image market. Digital photos are so inexpensive to take that nonprofessional photographers who are in the right place at the right time are bound to capture great images, if for no other reason than the law of large numbers.[32]

The rapid market embrace of digital photography also caught Kodak off guard. Not only had Kodak not anticipated how quickly the market would go digital, the terrorist attacks of September 11, 2001, decimated leisure travel and the picture taking that goes with it. Even as post-9/11 travel returned to normal levels, film purchases declined 10 to 15 percent annually in subsequent years. This was a one-two punch that almost sank the company, requiring it to resort to massive layoffs to meet its financial obligations and free up resources it could commit to funding investments in digital research. In 2004, Kodak announced a four-year, $3.4 billion restructuring plan that included the elimination of some fifteen thousand employees worldwide and more than forty of its photofinishing labs.[33]

To its credit, within four years, Kodak offset its double-digit declines in film sales with double-digit sales increases of digital cameras, retail-kiosk photo printing, digital picture frames, and inkjet printers.[34] The company expects the inkjet printer business alone to generate $1 billion in annual revenue by 2010. Still, changing dynamics can come from anywhere: Kodak's sales of movie film dropped 7 percent in the fourth quarter of 2007 because of a Hollywood writers' strike.[35]

New technologies, changing buying patterns, and an ever-evolving consumer culture have challenged once-high-flying companies from Tupperware to Motorola and Sharper Image to AT&T. Changing dynamics have been a boon to the economy on a macro level but often at the expense of individual companies.

Of course, there's another side to the story. As you have undoubtedly noticed, for every company that is blindsided and undermined by unpredictable change, there's another company that takes advantage of it. Many of the great investment windfalls of history— the monster hits that farsighted portfolio managers consistently search for—involve companies poised to enjoy huge growth when changing dynamics make their innovations the hottest properties on the planet.

Harold Levy is the portfolio manager of the First Eagle Fund of America, an equity fund that invests in companies affected by "catalysts causing positive corporate change not previously recognized by the market." "When there is change," Levy says, "there is a misunderstanding to be capitalized on."[36] He's right. First Eagle Fund generated an impressive 13.6 percent average annual return in the two decades since its inception in 1987: $10,000 invested at its launch turned into more than $135,000 twenty years later, nearly double the performance of Standard & Poor's 500.

There's a reason why "the only thing constant is change" is a cliché. It's true.

Riding the Tectonic Waves

The external factors we've examined in this chapter are never going to go away. In the years to come, the economy is going to expand and contract. Competition will come and go. And the dynamics of every industry will continue to shift. As Peter Kenny, managing director at Knight Capital Group, aptly characterized the fallout from the credit crunch, "The tectonic plates beneath the world financial system are shifting, and there is going to be a new financial world order that will be born of this."[37]

Sitting behind your desk dealing with the day-to-day challenges of business, it can be hard to notice changes that take months or years to gather force. But like the hands of a clock, factors that affect business keep moving. One day you may look up and see that your company's time of growth has (at least temporarily) passed.

The good news is that every company, including your competition, has to cope with market tectonics. When the ground shifts, it shakes everyone. The difference between companies that are able to grow for the long term and those that struggle, we have found, is not how hard market tectonics have hit them; it's how well they've dealt with the aftermath.

As you will see in the coming pages, tectonic events often reveal fissures within a company's internal environment that present the biggest challenges to overcoming a stall. Like roaches that scatter when the light comes on, these characteristics hide inside companies, leaving evidence of their existence even as they go unrecognized. Whether it's a debilitating lack of consensus, a loss of nerve among top management, a lack of focus in the marketplace, or inconsistency of execution (and sometimes all of the above), these dynamics can ruin a company from the inside out. Recognizing their existence and understanding their effects are the first steps toward getting back on the growth curve.

4

Lack of Consensus

As long as an organization is enjoying healthy growth, it seems that management can do no wrong. But when tectonics shift and growth begins to stall, internal rifts can become apparent. People choose sides, challenge each other, question long-held assumptions, and begin to doubt strategies and tactics that used to be sacrosanct. Such internal discord can paralyze efforts to mount an effective recovery.

We first discovered this issue in the pilot study about company growth that we completed back in 2001. The issue of internal consensus wasn't yet on our radar screen; in our advertising practice, we had seen that the most effective companies seemed to be headed by a strong, visionary CEO who single-handedly set the strategic direction for the entire organization, and we took that model somewhat for granted. (We were not the only ones to take that perspective. Judging by the way business magazines, TV news programs, book publishers, and others continue to lionize the supposedly heroic do-it-all CEO, the myth that successful corporations are essentially piloted by soloists is alive and well.)

Since then, however, we have examined the data from two comprehensive nationwide studies, analyzed the histories of many stalled companies, and talked to executives at every level of organizations, both successful and not so successful. As a result, we've reached the conclusion that a lack of consensus is the number one internal problem facing stalled growth companies.

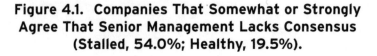

Figure 4.1. Companies That Somewhat or Strongly Agree That Senior Management Lacks Consensus (Stalled, 54.0%; Healthy, 19.5%).

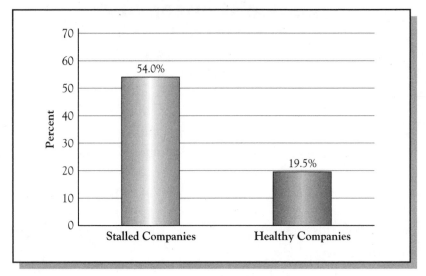

What Is Consensus?

Acknowledging the crucial role consensus plays in business can be difficult because "consensus" itself is a term that's often derided. Britain's "Iron Lady" prime minister Margaret Thatcher once said, "Consensus is the absence of leadership," and she has been quoted by politicians and pundits alike to make a point about the need for leaders to be willing to make bold decisions and, if necessary, stand against the tide. Sometimes that sort of boldness is necessary. But in most circumstances, the most effective political leaders are those who build on a mandate provided by the voters—"mandate" being, in effect, another word for consensus. Those who neglect the power and importance of consensus may find themselves impotent or (in a parliamentary system) out on their ear, stripped of office by their disaffected former supporters.

It is important at the outset, therefore, to define what exactly we mean by consensus in a corporate context. First of all, it does not mean management by committee. Trying to get everybody to agree on everything is not leadership, it's a form of passivity. And it is impossible, to boot. What consensus does mean, in this context, is agreement among an organization's senior leadership about the nature and purpose of the company and where it's intended to go. And this agreement must be part of the bedrock on which the company is built, not something hastily forged when circumstances demand it. There are occasions when critical, time-sensitive decisions need to be made with little time for communication, let alone consensus building. Companies that have as part of their strategic foundation a general consensus on global issues are less likely to make mistakes when decisions are made under duress.

Second, consensus does not neglect the need for (or minimize the value of) a strong CEO. In those organizations that do benefit from companywide consensus, it is often the product of an inspired vision championed by a smart, charismatic leader. But the fact that such a leader tends to be the center of a company's solar system doesn't diminish the need for harmony of the planets in orbit around him or her. If that harmony is lacking, the CEO alone will not have the gravity to hold the company together.

Third, consensus does not mean agreement on every detail. Thatcher's quote is best understood in the context of defining historical moments in highly charged political environments, not the everyday operations of a close-knit team focusing on a strategic objective. While a military general needs to be willing to make bold decisions, the officers under the general must operate with clear consensus as to their broad objectives, or carnage will result. Each subordinate officer can use his professional skills and judgment during the heat of battle in the way he sees fit, but if the officers are not all focused on taking the same hill, their troops will be divided—and defeated.

In his best-selling book, *The Five Dysfunctions of a Team*, Patrick Lencioni points out that a company is much like an athletic team.[1] It may have a number of talented individuals, but if they all act on their own instincts, running in whatever direction seems best to them, they are likely to get beaten. The best teams take their moves out of a common playbook, and the more consensus they display in understanding and following it, the more likely they are to win the game.

As we zeroed in on stalled companies in our research, we saw the consensus principle at work. Managers of struggling companies were more than three times as likely as those in healthy organizations to admit that they were experiencing internal discord and couldn't make critical decisions. They were more than four times as likely to say that they and their colleagues were moving in different directions. And they were six times less likely to report that they knew where their company was going. These struggling companies were simply paralyzed by a lack of consensus. That's why we put consensus issues at the top of the list of internal factors that must be overcome when growth stalls. That and what we witness every day both in our own practice and the business press.

Figure 4.2. Companies That Somewhat or Strongly Agree That "We Can't Seem to Make a Decision" (Stalled, 40.0%; Healthy, 11.5%).

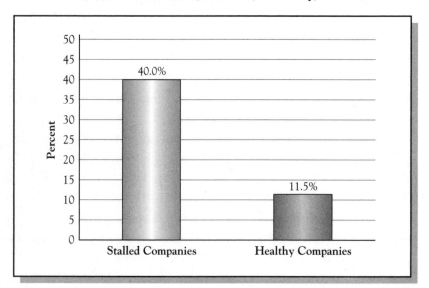

Zippo is a good case in point. For years Zippo owned the dominant market share in the growing and dependable refillable-lighter business. But Zippo ran into a destructive dynamic as societal norms increasingly turned against smoking. As fewer people took up the habit, fewer people had the need for refillable lighters.

The company's chairman, George Duke, was the grandson of Zippo's founder. One of his challenges was corralling the five other family members who owned equal shares of the company's stock and had their own ideas about what Zippo should do about its troubles, from sticking to its refillable-lighter guns to selling flashlights, money clips, and even watches. As Duke put it, "It was difficult to come to a consensus in a timely manner. It was very hard to embark on a strategy." As a result, Zippo's sales stalled for several years.[2]

French retail giant Carrefour seems to have learned from Zippo's example. The world's second-largest retailer, with more than fifteen thousand hypermarkets, supermarkets, discount outlets, and convenience stores in thirty countries, Carrefour had been run for nearly a decade by the Halley family, which through a special voting bloc controlled 20 percent of the company's voting rights. But in the rapidly changing and hotly competitive retail world, Carrefour found itself increasingly challenged by the aggressive expansion and price cutting of rivals (including its one larger global competitor, Walmart).

As with the Duke family at Zippo, various Halley family members had their own ideas about how to best manage the competitive challenges; some wanted out of the company altogether but were prevented from exiting owing to the nature of the voting bloc. Family feuds were a distraction Carrefour could ill afford, and the family wisely agreed to dissolve its alliance and give up two seats on the supervisory board. Now Halley family members are treated in the same way as regular shareholders and can sell their stock at will. The change makes it easier for the company to assemble a board that shares a common vision for the company's future, such as pursuing faster growth in China and other emerging markets, funded by selling Carrefour's real estate assets.[3]

The business world is littered with examples of companies that through a lack of consensus became their own worst enemies. The failure of the Daimler-Chrysler merger can be blamed at least in part on a lack of consensus at the most fundamental level of corporate culture. When Juergen Schrempp, Daimler-Chrysler CEO and architect of the merger, was asked a year into the union what he thought the oddest thing about Americans was, he said, "It's that at lunch they drink iced tea and ice water," instead of the wine to which employees in Stuttgart were accustomed.[4] USA Today quoted a professor at Tufts University's law and diplomacy school, Jeswald Salacuse, who pointed out that the company's German and American executives could not even agree on minor issues, saying they "spent a lot of time wrangling about the size of the new company's business card."[5] These sorts of minor cultural differences reflected broader, deeper disagreements over issues ranging from brand development to technology sharing to pricing, leading to the company's failure.[6]

Burger King is another company that has struggled with consensus for decades. The chain went through ten CEOs over a fifteen-year period, hired five different advertising agencies in less than ten years, and suffered through seven consecutive years of declining sales.[7] What would cause a company to play such an extended and destructive game of management musical chairs? A lack of consensus among the franchisee community. What ailed Burger King over the years wasn't a lack of ideas from the parade of CEOs and ad agencies. They simply couldn't come to sustained agreement as a company on a clear direction.

To their credit, in recent years Burger King has achieved a nice run of same-store sales growth credited to a smart menu strategy and creative campaign targeting their core of young male heavy users. But the test will be to see if the owner-operators can stay the course when they run over the next speed bump or if they again dump their management team and start over.

Interestingly, the advertising agency that finally gave Burger King its winning formula, Crispin Porter + Bogusky, didn't fare so well with Miller Brewing. Crispin's "Man Laws" campaign for

Miller Lite was initially popular among distributors but didn't ring the sales bell, and two months after Miller management pulled the plug on the campaign, the agency resigned the account. Commenting on the agency's unusual decision, Crispin's chief creative officer, Alex Bogusky, said in a statement, "Although we made every attempt to find common ground, the process of multilayered approvals of creative strategy has made doing work we can be proud of increasingly difficult." An unnamed industry observer was quoted in *Advertising Age* as saying of Miller, "You've got three or four different top-tier people with contradictory points of view. There's a constant shifting of strategy and a lack of a common vision."[8]

Before Carly Fiorina could even warm her seat as the new CEO of HP, she announced a bold plan to merge with Compaq Computers. Her vision ultimately resulted in a larger, more powerful HP, which enabled the company to overtake its biggest rival, Dell. But Fiorina wasn't there to take any bows because of the bitter public struggle the merger announcement kicked off between HP's new management team and its old guard.

David W. Packard, son of company founder Dave Packard and member of the HP board from 1987 to 1999, was desperately afraid that the merger with Compaq would forever alter the consensus-driven approach by which the company had been managed since inception, famously known as "the HP Way." He felt so strongly about the impact of the merger on HP's culture that he took out full-page ads in the major business press to denounce it. In one, he quoted at length from a 1960 speech by his father that cut to the chase of the disagreement:

> You know that those people you work with that are working only for money are not making any real contribution. I want to emphasize then that people work to make a contribution, and they do this best when they have a real objective, when they know what they are trying to achieve and are able to use their own capabilities to the greatest extent. This is a basic philosophy which we have discussed before—Management by Objective as compared to Management by Control.

In other words, when we discuss supervision and management, we are not talking about a military type organization where the man at the top issues an order and it is passed on down the line until the man at the bottom does as he is told without question (or reason). That is precisely the type of organization we do not want. We feel our objectives can best be achieved by people who understand what they are trying to do and can utilize their own capabilities to do them.[9]

Packard titled his advertisement, "A Day at the Old HP." When the deal with Compaq closed, Packard lost his battle, but it's telling that not even half of HP's employees ended up supporting the merger. When Fiorina resigned under fire in 2005, it was clear that, regardless of the wisdom of her strategy, she'd lost the war.[10]

That's the biggest problem underlying issues of consensus in struggling companies: they are symptomatic of a loss of trust and respect for the management team. Our research demonstrates that this is a common and often crippling problem among companies that have stalled.

In January 2007, the CEOs of two of the largest candy makers in the world, Cadbury and Hershey, were near an agreement to merge and create a powerful global candy empire. But less than a year later, the deal was scrapped, and Hershey's CEO, along with eight former directors of the company, abruptly resigned or were dismissed. The CEO, Richard Lenny, was accused of withholding information from the Hershey Trust (established decades ago by company founder Milton Hershey), a charitable organization that controls 78 percent of the shareholder vote and for whose benefit the Hershey Company is supposed to be run. Trustees had seen the value of their holdings decline by more than $1 billion in the years leading up to the merger discussions and didn't like what they perceived as the secretive nature of the talks. One Hershey, Pennsylvania, newspaper called the sudden changing of the guard "the Sunday night massacre."

In its postmortem, here's how the *Wall Street Journal* described the mess: "Hershey's downward spiral offers an illustration of how a breakdown in communication and trust among a company's main actors—management, the board of directors, and key shareholders—can paralyze an organization and leave it vulnerable. As Hershey Trust Chairman LeRoy Zimmerman wrote in an October letter to Hershey Co.'s board: 'The lifeblood of collaboration is truth.'"[11] Ouch.

No Consensus? No Surprise

The fact that all management teams tend to struggle with consensus shouldn't be surprising. Although management is an art, it is based on scientific principles, and we know from the second law of thermodynamics that energy always tends to flow from concentration to diffusion; in other words, hot things don't stay hot, and cold things don't stay cold. While a company isn't a physical object like a stove top or a refrigerator, it is composed of objects (both inert and alive) that are subject to the principle of entropy: all systems tend to break down. It's as true of corporations as it is of cornflakes that wilt and get soggy in a bowl of milk.

Sometimes success itself is the problem, causing rapidly growing companies to implode under their own weight. As a senior manager at Muni Financial Services, an acquaintance I'll call Frank had a front-row seat to the decline of the consulting firm. Muni Financial provided services and software to help cities, counties, and small municipalities service bond issues. The company hit a market sweet spot and had grown by leaps and bounds in the four-year period before Frank arrived. But the growth became too much for them, causing customer service issues, staffing problems, and turnover (which served dual roles as both cause and effect of the company's problems).

"You had new people coming in who had all kinds of ideas," Frank remembers, "and the people [who] were there had ideas. So what happened is you had this huge consensus issue." He recalls how the environment went from bad to worse: "We had management style issues, company culture clashes. . . . [It] was quite a roller coaster. The level of trust really started breaking down. I think that's probably the most fundamental part of this. When the level of trust breaks down, you don't know why you're doing what you're doing and who you can trust. I mean, everybody gets squirrelly. Who is a loyal subject? Who is a renegade? A lot of people became angry."

Frank left and joined a competitor, and Muni Financial was ultimately sold to a larger concern. Looking back, Frank now reflects, "It was clear that there wasn't a management consensus. If you really step back from it, I think a lot of people felt that they were part of the strategic management group and then realized that they weren't. When you're putting your all into something—you're responsible for something—and then you feel like it's a charade, it's an uncomfortable and very disappointing situation."

Muni Financial's growth was simply too much for its management structure to handle. The company added too many people who had ideas of their own, and offered no way to effectively integrate their perspectives. The level of trust broke down. While that's a problem that may show up in cases of too-rapid organic growth, it's almost inevitable when a company generates growth through mergers and acquisitions. Analysts and management teams are great at crunching the numbers but often fail to account for consensus-killing culture clashes.

When Internet portal Excite merged with online access provider@Home in a multibillion-dollar 1999 deal, the company thought it had what it needed to overtake AOL and Yahoo! and dominate the information superhighway. But by 2001, Excite@Home had declared bankruptcy. There were a number of reasons, from failed acquisitions to competitor countermoves, but former Excite@ Home CEO Tom Jermoluk put it more bluntly: "Quite simply, the company needed the support of its partners and never got it, because everyone had their own agendas." Stories in the press after the bankruptcy filing told tales of the internal arguments and board-room tussles to which Jermoluk refers.[12]

As long as a company achieves manageable growth, consensus issues tend to keep a low profile. But when the organization finds itself trying to integrate a new partner, or when tectonics shift and the company is facing a recession, a disruptive dynamic, or an aggressive competitor, divisions begin to appear. Factions often arise: newcomers versus old-timers, sales versus operations, headquarters versus the field, and so on. People begin to raise long-latent issues and challenge the way the organization does things. Strongly held opinions, based on differing backgrounds, experiences, and perspectives, confuse the picture. Before you know it, meetings are filled with strife as disagreements over priorities and strategy take center stage.

That's what our stalled growth revealed was happening at my own firm. As long as things were good, we set aside (or simply ignored) our personal and strategic differences and focused on the work. But when we ran into rough waters, our differing perspectives couldn't be ignored. The conflict they caused was both distracting and disturbing. And highly unproductive.

Consensus Is Vital

Because it's a "soft" virtue, difficult to spell out in a business plan or track in a profit-and-loss report, most companies underestimate the impact that a lack of consensus can have. When growth stalls and they drift along, unable to support a single direction for any length of time, they may blame the economy, the competition, or the person in the office down the hall, without realizing that the problem is more systemic than that.

The first step in getting back up to speed is coming to an understanding that the key people on your team all need to be heading in the same direction. My firm uses a proprietary strategic planning process to help companies overcome destructive internal dysfunctions while addressing the unique marketplace dynamics they face. Step one of the process both requires and ensures that they develop consensus around key issues. This is especially vital in our somewhat subjective field of integrated marketing communications. Too many times we have witnessed how easily a lack of consensus can derail the effort.

Mary Thompson, president of Mr. Rooter Plumbing (and one of our clients), agrees. She related to me a story about the keynote speakers at the 2006 International Franchise Association convention, Ralph Alvarez, president of McDonald's North America, and Reggie Webb, president of McDonald's Leadership Council. Having worked with many clients in the fast-food industry, I know that it's not always easy for corporate folks and the franchise community to agree. But Mary was impressed with how Webb and Alvarez emphasized the importance of unity in taking care of the customer. They said they can't afford to "agree to disagree"; they may debate about the best way to achieve their goals, but by the time they leave the room, they need to have achieved consensus on a common approach. That may be one reason why, through good times and bad, McDonald's tends to keep a leg up on its competitors.

That's also how a great company like San Jose–based eBay can keep from missing a beat even after the worst terrorist attacks in history. On 9/11, eBay's able CEO, Meg Whitman, was half a world away in Japan. Her chief operating officer, Brian Swette, was in Florida, all the way across the country from headquarters. Because U.S. airspace was shut down, neither could hop on the next flight home. But Whitman wasn't worried. "By the time I was able to call in, our team was already thinking about and acting on the big issues," she said. "I did not have to say anything for the right thing to happen." Whitman had done an amazing job in creating consensus among the then-twenty-five-hundred employees she had grown the company to (from a mere thirty-five when she came on board).[13]

Wayne Rosing, vice president of engineering at Google during its early growth years from 2001 to 2005, described a similar culture at his highly focused company: "For a while I had 160 direct reports. No managers. It worked because the teams knew what they had to do. That set a cultural bit in people's heads: You are the boss. Don't wait to take the hill. Don't wait to be managed."[14] Google's mission, technology, and even its "Don't be evil" mantra—which faces increasing scrutiny as the company has transitioned from underdog to behemoth—has provided almost a cultlike sense of consensus within the company.

Compare Google's internal consensus with the culture clashes at Home Depot, the postmerger disaster that is Sprint Nextel, or the yearlong battle between Ed Zander the (now-former) CEO of Motorola and corporate raider Carl Icahn, who wanted a seat on the board and a say in the strategy of the struggling company. Until that issue was resolved, it didn't matter who was right and who was wrong; the consensus issue itself was debilitating. Energy that should have been spent overcoming Motorola's tectonic issues was used up in the boardroom.

Is something similar happening in your company? Is there unresolved conflict or a lack of trust or respect among your management team? Are your people harboring unspoken doubts or undermining one another in passive-aggressive ways? If so, ignoring the problem isn't the answer. It won't go away. In Chapter 9, I will begin to outline the steps your company can take to ensure that a strong consensus exists around the key challenges you face. I'll also explain what you can do if you discover that you are already dealing with a lack-of-consensus problem.

The late Peter Drucker, perhaps history's single greatest management thinker, summed up the importance of consensus this way: "Results are obtained only by concentration of resources, especially by concentration of the scarcest and most valuable resource, people with proven performance capacity."[15] If your people don't have proven performance capacity, that's issue number one. But if they do, their efforts need to be concentrated. If they disagree with each other (or with you), get it out on the table. The answers may not be easy or apparent (if they were, you would have discovered them already), but admitting you have a consensus problem enables you to clear the deck of phony allegiances to failing strategies. Then together you can go to work uncovering the genuine issues your company is facing.

Do You Suffer a Lack of Consensus?

Consensus issues are hard to identify and unpleasant to face. But if you have a consensus problem, things can't get better until you recognize it. See how many of the following questions to which you can honestly answer "yes." And don't stop there. Ask your leadership team to honestly assess its answers as well. If you all tend to answer the questions positively, you're probably in pretty good shape. But if the answers are "no"—or you can't even agree on them—shut the door and admit there's a problem. With consensus on that, you can start working toward the solution.

- Do the members of your company's leadership team respect and trust one another?
- Do you have confidence in one another and in the company's plan?
- Are you all moving in the same direction?
- Are you all fully aligned on strategy?
- Do you operate like a well-oiled machine?
- Is it "one for all, all for one" in your company?
- Do you resolve your disagreements through open discussion, or does dissent fester?
- Can you make key corporate decisions confidently, knowing that the other members of the team will support you?
- Do you agree on where you are and where you're going as a company?

5

Loss of Focus

In early 2005, rumors were swirling that legendary retailer Neiman Marcus was on the block. In March of that year, investment bankers were predicting a price in the $4 billion range based on the company's stock price, which had recently seen double-digit increases and was hovering in the mid-$80s. But one analyst cautioned that with its gains, the company would be harder to sell because, in his mind, the market for luxury items might have peaked. His exact words were, "Neiman Marcus is skating on thin ice."[1]

So much for thin ice. In less than sixty days, Neiman Marcus announced a deal whereby shareholders would cash out at $100 per share, based on a total purchase price of $5.1 billion. Why the premium price? Kewsong Lee, a managing director at Warburg Pincus, one of the firms involved in the buyout, gave a simple explanation: "Burt Tansky and the management team have done a phenomenal job in keeping Neiman Marcus focused on its core strengths. The company has enjoyed record operating and financial performance, and we look forward to working with Burt and his team to continue building upon this track record of success."[2]

Focus. For one hundred years, it has been Neiman Marcus's strength, through good times and bad. After the terrorist attacks of 2001, when competitors like Saks and Gucci reacted to the economic uncertainty with lower prices, Neiman Marcus held its ground. Although same-store sales were down 4.4 percent in 2002, in 2003 they were back into positive territory and in 2004 made an incredible jump of nearly 15 percent. The company and its buyers were determined that the acquisition wasn't going to change a thing.

Tansky, the longtime Neiman Marcus CEO, said at the time, "We're going to maintain the same discipline we always have. Our new partners are anxious to make certain that we continue to do what we do well."[3]

And they have. Neiman Marcus's same-store sales growth in the years following the buyout remained in the 6 to 7 percent range. Based on its successful track record, the company is unlikely to let sales dips caused by recent economic gyrations or any other tectonic event change its winning formula.

Yes, you may say, but we're not Neiman Marcus; my company doesn't operate in the exciting market of luxury goods. That's exactly the point. There's only one Neiman Marcus because Neiman Marcus focuses so well on its strengths. Focus is an essential strategy for every company, even in the most mundane of industries.

When Dan Amos took the reins of Aflac, he became the leader of a company in an obscure segment (long-term disability) of a boring industry (insurance) headquartered in an out-of-the-way place (Columbus, Georgia). Aflac was, at that time, almost unheard of in the United States, doing most of its business in Japan. But Amos set out to change things, and to do so he knew he had to focus—both his message and his resources. He sold the company's businesses in eight countries to fund a consumer advertising push, the beginning of a brand-development program that ultimately led to the Aflac duck, one of the most successful advertising icons in history. The laserlike focus Amos and his team displayed in taking Aflac from a no-name insurance company to one of the best-known brands in business has provided shareholders a return of nearly 4,000 percent over his eighteen-year tenure. Amos himself boasted in 2008 that Aflac is "making over a million dollars an hour in profit."[4]

Unfortunately, not every company is able to marshal the will to focus like that, especially when growth stalls. Our research shows that companies whose growth has gone flat are five times more likely than healthy companies to have lost their focus. Pause and think about that statistic for a moment: *five times* more likely to have lost their focus.

**Figure 5.1. Companies That Somewhat or Strongly Agree
That "We've Lost Focus" (Stalled, 35%; Healthy, 7%).**

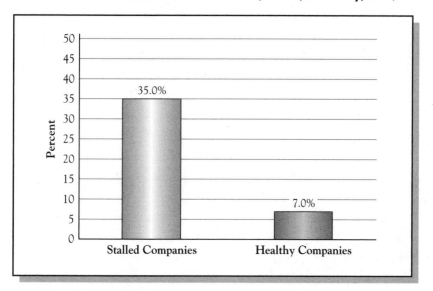

There's a simple reason why focus is so essential. No matter how big the company, its management team has only a finite amount of resources—money, time, talent, energy—at its disposal. The less focused those resources become, the less muscle management can muster to move the company forward or, if necessary, pull it out of a ditch. It's not unlike swinging a baseball bat: if your hips are going one way and your arms another, the ball's not going to go far. And if you don't keep your eyes focused on your target, you'll miss it altogether.

Every business leader I speak with understands the importance of this principle. Yet often companies lose their focus. Why? Just as in hitting a baseball, maintaining strategic focus takes intense concentration and the relentless elimination of distractions. If it were easy to do, a lot fewer companies would stumble (and the Baseball Hall of Fame would be packed with .400 hitters).

Even the most sophisticated companies struggle in this area. McDonald's has been the world's largest hamburger chain for more than fifty years, and (as noted in Chapter 2) has ridden out a tectonic event or two. Yet in 2001 and 2002, McDonald's went backward in the United States as same-store sales went in the tank.

A preoccupation with international expansion had distracted McDonald's from the operational excellence for which it had been famous, and the customers it had taken for granted found more interesting food, cleaner stores, and better experiences elsewhere. As CEO Jim Skinner described it in the company's 2002 annual report, McDonald's had been too intent on "adding restaurants to customers" rather than "adding customers to restaurants." Oddly, McDonald's pursuit of growth is what led to its stall.

That's when Skinner met with his chief lieutenants and developed the "Plan to Win," a blueprint for how to pull the company out of its doldrums. The core idea was to refocus the company on what it had historically done best. Skinner put it bluntly at the time: "Look, we've got to do a better job of delivering what we called quality, service, and cleanliness on a daily basis in our restaurants." The company went back to its roots, slowed the growth of new stores, boosted marketing spending, and focused all its energy on trying to become a better McDonald's.

It worked, and McDonald's went on a several-year run of same-store sales growth. The advice Skinner gives to people faced with the need to turn a company around reflects both the consensus and focus principles: "Have a plan of action. Stick with it, align your team around it, and focus on execution."[5]

How do companies get into unfocused messes? Why is it that, despite innumerable examples of those who have gone before and failed, management teams continue to lose their focus? Bain & Company's James Allen and Chris Zook, authors of *Profit from the Core*, say, "It's almost as if most growth strategies harbor a dark, destructive force that causes companies to reduce their focus on their core business and thereby to depart from the basis of their real differentiation."[6] Our research reveals that the "dark, destructive force" manifests itself in two ways: either the market moves, or the company does.

When the Market Moves

Imagine you're studying a fascinating bit of protoplasm under a powerful microscope. The heavy base on which the microscope sits ensures that it stays firmly grounded on the table, and its giant gears allow the lens mechanism to gently glide up and down with precision. With just a few small adjustments, the device enables you to focus tightly on the object of your interest.

Until an earthquake hits, that is. Microscopes are designed to withstand the small bumps and jiggles they may encounter in normal laboratory conditions, but if the ground starts shaking, all bets are off. The likelihood is pretty good that when it's all over, you'll have to refocus the instrument, if not pick it up off the ground and put it back together again. A similar effect can happen to happily focused companies when hit with a tectonic event.

Sometimes the impact is slow and gradual, like the shifting retail landscape that knocked Sears off its place atop the retail pyramid. Building on its trusted reputation as the catalogue merchant of choice in the early part of the last century, Sears was a department store pioneer and the only game in town across much of the United States. I vividly remember paging through the toy section of the Sears catalogue as a child in anticipation of what I might find under the Christmas tree.

But slowly, the characteristics of the marketplace in which Sears built its dominant position began to change. Population increases in towns where Sears had been the leading (if not the only) department store attracted competitors. Rising wages and the advent of the two-earner family provided additional disposable income that Sears' customers could spend with more upscale merchants. The traffic that Sears helped generate to large, regional malls where the stores served as anchors enabled smaller, specialized retailers to gain a foothold in almost every category, from clothing to appliances to electronics. New catalogue retailers took advantage of the comfort consumers felt (thanks largely to Sears' dependability) ordering through the mail by offering deep selections of narrowly focused merchandise.

And the bigger Walmart and Target grew, the greater their pricing power became, enabling them to catch and overtake Sears in trust, affordability, and convenience to consumers.

None of these effects is solely responsible for the decline of Sears. But looking back over the past half-century, they collectively changed the marketplace so much that Sears was left without an oar in the water. The company has been drifting for the past few decades.

Sears didn't change, the marketplace did. And just as a distant ship that is traveling against the horizon will gradually slip out of sight, the focus that had once enabled Sears to dominate its category slipped away, despite the company's own fidelity to its once-successful vision.

A similar, slow-moving devolution happened to Tidy Cat, the dominant brand in the cat litter category. In the 1990s, competitive tectonics began eroding the brand's market share as new players built compelling identities around distinctive product features such as odor control or scooping litter. Before they knew it, Tidy Cat led in only two of eighteen cat litter image attributes, and both revolved around price. The brand was being squeezed into commodity status.

But in this case, company leadership recognized what was happening and took steps to respond effectively. Sales results showed that one product line was still showing signs of strength: Tidy Cat Multiple Cat formula. Through significant research, the company came to the conclusion that the brand could be refocused toward an even narrower segment than its traditional cat owner customers: people who owned multiple cats. Tidy Cat boldly changed everything about the brand, including its advertising, its media strategy, its packaging, and even its name. Tidy Cat became Tidy Cats.

It worked. In the six years following the launch of the new focus, Tidy Cats' sales grew from $215 million to over $400 million. Significantly, among its target audience, the brand also took the number one spot in all eighteen category image attributes.[7]

Faced with the same problem as Sears—a shifting market throwing its brand identity out of focus—Tidy Cat management responded by sharpening its focus on a narrower, more profitable target. This is one effective way to respond when market evolution slowly degrades the potency of your brand's appeal.

Sometimes the tectonic changes are more noticeable. This happened when IBM saw its dominance in mainframe computers become less relevant each year as PCs increasingly took over their tasks. And it happened when Applebee's, the largest casual dining chain in the United States, allowed competitors like Chili's and Friday's to closely mimic its formula.

Occasionally the marketplace tectonics move so swiftly and significantly that it's hard to know what to do. The Internet changed many industry models overnight, including bookstores (Amazon), music (iTunes), movie rentals (Netflix), Yellow Pages (Yahoo!), and classified ads (craigslist). In each case, incumbent companies that once dominated their markets have been left scrambling to refocus. Some are coping well; others will become permanent casualties.

When the Company Moves

A loss of focus can't always be blamed on the shifting sands of the market. More often than not, it's the fault of the company. Unfortunately, the ill effects of a gradual loss of focus are not always readily apparent, which makes the problem difficult to recognize and address.

Years ago I was a passenger in a vehicle that got into a head-on collision. Mercifully, everyone in our car walked away from the crash. I thought I had escaped unscathed until I awoke the next morning; every bone in my body ached. That's how it is with a loss of focus—feeling fine today doesn't mean that the consequences aren't coming down the road.

Excite@Home failed in part because of a lack of consensus among key players on its management team. But before the merger even happened, Excite had passed on a tremendous opportunity. Robert Cringely, an early adviser to the company, told the story in *Inc.* magazine of how Excite lost—or perhaps missed altogether— its original focus:

One reason Excite and so many other Internet businesses from the 1990s stumbled was that they saw their original business idea not as an end but as a means. Excite had the best searching technology of its day, but the company saw searching as a steppingstone on the way to becoming the Internet equivalent of a television network. Searching would attract users, but what would keep them was to turn the search engine into a portal on the Web. At least that was the idea. So Excite, Yahoo!, and others added staff and increased expenditures, driven by the idea that searching alone wouldn't be enough to sustain a significant Internet enterprise. They were wrong.[8]

Yes, Excite was wrong, but that's easy for any of us to say in hindsight. It would have been harder at the time to recognize the immense potential value of a great search engine, which is why the founders of Google deserve enormous credit for their foresight. In a 2001 profile on the company, the *Wall Street Journal* reported that "Google executives say they don't expect to go in the direction of offering the cornucopia of email and other services that Yahoo!, America Online, or MSN provide—primarily because they don't want to compete in that crowded field. Instead, Google will continue to focus on search." The article quoted Google cofounder Larry Page as saying, "We try to keep it simple. We try to give you exactly what you want."[9] Staying focused made Page and his partner Sergey Brin very, very rich men.

Loss of focus can be caused by many things, from boredom to fear, egoism to opportunism, or just plain greed. Unfortunately, there are plenty of examples of each. H&R Block is the leading name in the tax business and the closest thing to a recession-proof business there is. The tax deadline of April 15 comes every year, regardless of economic conditions, and the more the federal government complicates the tax code, the better it is for business. (When I worked as an intern for the Senate Budget Committee in 1985, the tax code numbered 26,300 pages. Today it numbers 67,200.[10]) But the company couldn't avoid the temptation of getting in on the exploding subprime mortgage business. When the meltdown began in 2007, H&R Block's Option One Mortgage dragged corporate earnings down with it. Richard Breeden, a former Securities and Exchange Commission chairman who became H&R Block's CEO in late 2007, rectified the problem by selling the unit, saying, "We've capped the well."[11] Within months, the company returned to profitability and again saw double-digit revenue increases.[12]

Charles Schwab and Company carved out a valuable niche in the last quarter of the twentieth century serving individual investors. Founder Charles Schwab himself says, "Originally, I was aiming for a very small segment of the population: sophisticated, self-directed investors who wanted someone to execute their trades efficiently and economically, without salesmanship, interference, or intimidation."[13] The company took off in the 1990s when the tech boom created a whole new class of investors who fit the Schwab mold (myself included).

But when the economy went sour in 2000, so did Schwab's business, and the company tried a number of things to overcome declining revenues. Schwab, who had retired in 1999, came back in 2004 to resurrect his company, publicly saying Charles Schwab and Company had lost its focus.[14] He cut costs by closing branches, reducing staff, and exiting the capital markets business so the company could reduce its trading prices by as much as two-thirds to again make it more accessible to individual investors.[15] Of that time, Schwab said, "We reaffirmed our single-minded strategic focus on individual investors and the advisors who serve them." The move paid off, with revenues growing faster than the economy in 2006 and 2007, 19 percent and 16 percent, respectively.

Walmart has been the reason behind many companies' growth problems with its relentless focus on cost cutting and "always low prices" positioning. Doug Dean, head of the company's general merchandise division, describes Walmart's traditional customer in simple terms: "the people who live paycheck to paycheck."[16] But on June 6, 2005, a small, seven-paragraph story in the *Wall Street Journal* caught my eye. The headline read, "Walmart's Chief Says Retailer Needs to Widen Customer Appeal." The article went on to explain that Walmart was still doing reasonably well, with same-store sales increases up 2.5 percent in recent months, but that wasn't good enough. Lee Scott, CEO, said, "We need to widen our appeal to a broader range of customer."[17]

That's it, I thought. Walmart blinked.

I didn't think it could happen, that a company that was always so focused on what it did better than anybody else could give into the temptation to get fuzzy. Was it the tough expectations of analysts? The brutal competition from stylish (and pesky) Target? A loss of internal consensus? Whatever the case, while most analysts fawned over Walmart's newfound enlightenment, I wanted to go on record against it. So I wrote in a *BusinessWeek.com* column that they were making a mistake.[18]

Walmart relegated its campy smiley-faced icon to a backseat role, opting instead for tactics like a two-year deal with *Vogue* that included 116 full pages of ads, beginning with an eight-page spread in the September 2005 issue. Walmart CMO John Fleming said at the time, "We chose to team up with fashion authority *Vogue* to show the female consumer that dressing fashionably is now easier to achieve than ever before." He went on to say, "The message before was branding our low price message and telling our story as a company. Now we want to drive the product."[19]

I can just hear the conversations now at a fancy cocktail party:

"I love your dress; it's beautiful!"
"Oh, thanks. Walmart, you know."

It was never going to happen. And it didn't. In the fiscal year that ended January 31, 2007, Walmart had its worst annual same-store sales growth in more than a decade.[20] Fleming was succeeded as CMO by Stephen Quinn, a senior vice president of marketing who had urged restraint in drifting from the low-price positioning.[21]

When it comes to losing focus, perhaps no industry tops the automakers. Here are just a few examples:

Volkswagen

After the success of the original "people's car" in the 1950s and 1960s, Volkswagen went on a long, slow decline in the United States. Sales dropped from 569,182 units in 1970 to under 100,000 units in the early 1990s. Although everybody fondly remembers the original VW Beetle, not many people have a warm spot in their heart for the Rabbit, launched by Volkswagen in the mid 1970s to combat affordable, dependable Japanese imports. John Slaven, former VW marketing director, captured the essence of VW's Rabbit problem when he said, "If American Motors had built the Rabbit, no one would have been surprised. But when VW built it, it was like a family member lying to you."[22]

In 1998 the company returned to its roots by introducing the new Beetle. VW dealers were thrilled, one saying, "We can't keep up with the flow. The new Beetle is like a magnet that draws people back to us." Sales shot up to a high of 352,765 units in 2000.[23] Then the trend downward began again, this time exemplified by a 2001 decision to go "up market" with a $67,000 luxury car called the Phaeton. By 2007, U.S. sales were back down to around 200,000 vehicles, and the Phaeton was dead, having sold just over 2,000 units before it was yanked from the market.[24] Undeterred, Volkswagen is aiming to ramp sales up once again through the launch of a bevy of dependable, affordable new models, but time will tell if the company can again dig itself out of its hole.[25] With a goal of more than tripling the number of vehicles it sells in the United States within ten years, temptations to chase market share will abound.[26]

Mercedes

Long known as one of the finest luxury brands in the world, Mercedes wasn't content with its share of the automotive pie. Mike Jackson, former president and CEO of Mercedes-Benz U.S.A., said, "When we asked who makes the best car, people answered Mercedes. Who has the best resale value? Mercedes. Who has the safest car? Mercedes. On and on, down the list, question after question, Mercedes."[27] In the early 1990s the company launched the more affordable C-Class in an attempt to take advantage of its reputation and broaden its market. The car sold well (not surprisingly, considering the equity the brand had built over a century), which further encouraged

Mercedes in its expansionist ways. But the loss of focus had some ill effects, the most notable being a significant and embarrassing drop-off in quality.

In 2002 Mercedes finished thirteenth on J. D. Power's survey of new vehicle quality. Tom Libby, director of industry analysis at J. D. Power, said at the time, "My personal opinion is that a brand such as Mercedes should be at the top. That's what people's expectations of the brand are."[28] But it was not to be. In 2003 not a single Mercedes-Benz model made the *Consumer Reports* "recommended" list,[29] and by 2005 the brand's customer loyalty ratings began to measurably slip as well.[30] The Mercedes unit, which accounted for more than half of Daimler-Chrysler's operating profit in 2003, contributed only 30 percent in 2004.[31] Yet, Mercedes continues to expand its lineup, offering fifteen different models from sedans to roadsters, coupes to convertibles, wagons to trucks. Are they decent vehicles? Sure. Do they represent what Mercedes used to mean? I don't see how they can.

Rance Crain, president of Crain Communications (which publishes industry bible *Automotive News*), said in a 2002 *Advertising Age* editorial, "'Unlike any other' is the tagline for Mercedes' new ad campaign. In reality, the cars are getting to be just like everybody else's."[32] How true.

Saturn

Launched in 1990 as "a different kind of car company," Saturn broke new ground in the way automobiles were sold in the United States. Its inviting showrooms, friendly salespeople, and no-haggle pricing strategy set it apart from every other automotive brand. Although its cars didn't offer features or styling that could be considered breakthrough, they were nice looking, reasonably priced, and supported by a brilliant advertising effort developed by the late Hal Riney, the creative genius behind the legendary wine-cooler pitchmen Bartles & Jaymes and Ronald Reagan's 1984 "Morning in America" campaign.

The brand took off. In 1992 Saturn ranked number one in new-car sales per retailer, the first time in more than a decade that a domestic manufacturer had captured that honor. That year it also topped the J. D. Power Customer Satisfaction Index. Sales reached a high of over 286,000 units in 1994. Customers so loved the cars that some became Saturn sales consultants, and in what Steve Shannon, Saturn's director of consumer marketing, dubbed the "mother of all event marketing programs," thousands of owners and their families flocked to the Saturn "Homecoming" in Spring Hill, Tennessee, to enjoy catfish, country music, and tours of the plant.[33]

But instead of sticking to its knitting, the parent company's DNA took over, and Saturn began introducing a raft of new models based on existing General Motors platforms. The purity of Saturn's brand identity also began to wane from neglect; in 2002 Saturn general manager Jill Lajdziak made clear that the company doesn't believe a focus on its retail experience is a sustainable strategy. "We have to make sure people love our product as much as the experience," she said, apparently oblivious to the fact that in many ways the experience *was* the product. Since its high-water mark, Saturn has been unable to recapture the magic that made the brand famous.[34]

Chrysler

In the early years of the new millennium, Chrysler was somewhat a victim of its failed decade as a subsidiary of Daimler-Chrysler. Analysts say that during that nine-year period, there was an emphasis on cost cutting at Chrysler, in part so that its vehicles could maintain some level of differentiation from Mercedes' down-market expansion. That affected Chrysler's quality perceptions, which were further damaged as suggested improvements had to make their way through the parent company's bloated bureaucracy. (In 2008, shortly after Daimler-Chrysler's divestiture, both the Chrysler and Dodge brands ranked below average in the J. D. Power quality survey, and the Jeep brand was at the bottom.[35]) The company also made the strange decision to tie its major brands together through a short-lived "Dr. Z" advertising campaign, featuring company chairman Dieter Zetsche touting the value of Mercedes' engineering heritage as an intended halo over Chrysler's stable of brands.

But the campaign helped neither Chrysler nor Mercedes, and by 2006 Chrysler's financial performance had declined so significantly that it became a critical drag on the overall company's results. Daimler looked for a way—any way—out.

When Cerberus Capital Management bought Chrysler in 2007, it had to contend with a lineup of some thirty vehicle models, excess dealer inventories, and a complex maze of internal cannibalization, as Chrysler's namesake models competed with similar offerings from siblings Jeep and Dodge.[36] In 2008 the company announced plans to eliminate up to half of its models, consolidate its dealer network, and make more money by focusing on producing fewer, better cars. "We're going to be the best little car company in America," said Jim Press, vice chairman.[37] But Chrysler continued to bleed cash, burdened by tectonic events in the broader economy, and was forced to turn its attention from success to simple survival.

The Michael Jordan Principle

Whether in the financial, retail, manufacturing, or any other sector, it's easy to oversimplify what are, in reality, complex business decisions. But the fact that management teams must navigate complexity reinforces the need for the simplifying effect of focus. Every company, like every baseball player, every astronaut, every attorney, and every physician, offers something of value. While that value may grow out of many different characteristics, those specialists will prosper only to the extent that they remain focused.

I call this the "Michael Jordan Principle." Michael Jordan is the greatest basketball player of all time and perhaps one of the greatest athletes of all time. Yet, even he couldn't make it in professional baseball. During 1994, his single experimental season as a Chicago White Sox farmhand, Jordan batted a disappointing .202 for the Birmingham Barons, hitting just three home runs and committing eleven errors. Was it because he didn't have the raw skills? I don't think so. I think the reason is simply that during all those years when Michael Jordan was focusing on basketball, his competitors on the diamond were focusing on baseball. To play at the highest levels of either sport—any sport—takes more than raw talent and an understanding of the game. It takes intense dedication and long-term focus.

It's no different at the highest levels of business. The Michael Jordan Principle suggests that you can be truly excellent at only one thing. Sometimes it takes a loss of focus to make a company realize what exactly its core strengths are.

So much has been written about Starbucks over the past few years that little more can be said about the company. Suffice it to say that even Howard Schultz admitted the company lost its focus during its rapid growth, selling breakfast sandwiches, peddling compact discs, and promoting movies, among other things.[38] "We desperately need to look in the mirror and realize it's time to get back to the core," he said in his now-famous leaked memo of 2007.[39]

Companies that lose focus forget what "brung 'em to the dance" and get distracted by other opportunities. Sometimes those opportunities manifest themselves in a temptation that provides an immediate lift to the top line: acquisitions.

The "A" Word

When organic growth isn't happening—or isn't happening enough—acquisitions can look awfully attractive. And acquisitions can serve an important strategic role, eliminating competition, streamlining back office and support functions, and providing quick economies of scale. Our research suggests that some level of acquisition activity can be beneficial, as long as it doesn't lead to a lack of consensus (culture clashes, infighting) or a loss of focus, in what the legendary investor Peter Lynch might call "diworseifications."[40]

One company that practices the right kind of acquisition strategy is Cisco Systems. Since the early 1990s, Cisco has pursued more than 125 acquisitions as a key pillar of its growth plan. Most of the companies Cisco acquires are small firms with industry-leading innovations related to Cisco's core networking equipment competency, almost as if the company is using the rapidly evolving technology marketplace as its external R&D department. Within sixty days of acquisition, Cisco ensures that the employees of each company are folded into the Cisco benefits and bonus plans, that clear lines of management leadership are developed and understood, and that sales functions are fully integrated. It's a formula that has helped the company rapidly grow to more than $35 billion in revenue. As Cisco acquires larger and larger companies, it will have a more challenging time digesting them, so time will tell if its formula holds up.[41]

Unfortunately, not all companies are as strategic, or as successful, with their acquisition strategies. When this happens, they often waste years in making ill-considered acquisitions, then selling them off, sometimes for less than they originally paid.

VeriSign, a leading provider of Internet services such as security programs and "digital certificates" that allow customers to shop online with confidence, announced in 2007 that it was going to start all over and "signal to the market that we are taking a different approach." (The words are those of Todd Johnson, vice president of broadband content services.) The company had acquired more than a dozen tech companies between 2004 and 2006 that Wall Street frowned on as providing too little synergy to the parent corporation. William Roper, VeriSign's CEO who is overseeing the divestitures of as many as ten companies acquired under his predecessor, admitted that the company lost its focus because of resource skirmishes among the different entities.[42]

Packaged-food companies are especially active in the acquisition-divestiture cycle, chasing the next hot product category or dumping brands past their prime. Nestlé, the world's biggest food company (but not its most profitable), in 2007 began trimming its product line, which has had as many as 130,000 variations.[43] Unilever, another global giant that lags in profitability, has been criticized for years by analysts for being too complex.[44] And H. J. Heinz has had as many as 100 brands and 250 legal entities to manage.[45]

Nelson Peltz, an activist Heinz shareholder who was also behind Cadbury Schweppes' spin-off of its Dr Pepper and Snapple subsidiaries (and whose Trian Fund Management also owns significant shares of Kraft Foods and Starbucks), said, "If you look at the best food companies in the world, they are all very focused."[46]

Acquisitions are an easy way to drive the top line, but they often cause consensus and focus issues that outweigh their benefits. They can even serve an enabling function to leaders of struggling companies who are in denial: as long as the company is getting larger, there's no problem, right? But there's a perverse logic in trying to combine two malfunctioning companies to make a better one. Anybody who's married understands that getting hitched doesn't hide your negative personality traits, it brings them to the surface. I never realized, for example, how selfish I was until I said "I do." (It happened again when I had kids, but that's another story.)

When tectonic events hit, they may reveal a lack of focus that has crept into your organization. Or they may be the cause of a loss of focus that arises out of a scramble for new revenue. But they can serve as a blessing as well, forcing you to come to grips with the true value your company provides to the marketplace. They can cause you to face up to your strengths and weaknesses and highlight (sometimes unmercifully) where you need to invest and where you must cut back. But as with a lack of consensus, the first step is to recognize that a loss of focus has occurred.

It's tempting, when growth stalls, to broaden your reach to a new industry or wider spectrum of customers. But it's rarely the answer. As one of the CEOs we interviewed said, you must "be very, very relevant to your market. Be clear on your core and what your place in the value chain is."

Have You Lost Your Focus?

Sometimes it's obvious that your company has lost focus, and the question is what to do about it (more on that later). But sometimes it's not so easy to tell. These questions may shed light on whether you have a focus problem—and how big of a challenge overcoming it might be.

- Can you state your company's core competency in simple terms?
- Can your employees state your company's core competency (and do their answers line up with yours)?
- Can you easily delineate the companies against which you compete?
- Do you know exactly who your prime prospects should be?
- Do internal tactical discussions regularly get elevated to complex strategic arguments?
- Are any of your employees or divisions working at cross-purposes?
- Do you struggle with where to allocate your marketing dollars?
- Is your research and development program productive, generating innovations that reinforce your company's core strengths?
- Do you have a simple, sensible, compelling elevator speech?
- Can you explain to your mother what your company does?

6

Loss of Nerve

We now look back on the late 1990s as the dot-com bubble, a heady time of wild innovation and rampant speculation. But back then, they were simply thought of as an unprecedented boom brought about by a healthy economy and the rise of the Internet. And when the bubble burst, companies like M^2 Consulting, then among the most successful growth businesses in America, had to find ways to cope with the fallout.

M^2 shrank from $25 million in revenue to $12 million in less than a year. Marion McGovern, the company's CEO, watched her firm's earnings fall from a positive $2 million to a negative half million over the same time period. Like the earthquakes that threaten her hometown of San Francisco, the bust shook the company—and her confidence—to the core.

"Everybody was shell-shocked," she remembers. Not only was M^2 itself struggling, its staff was largely paid on commission. Her people saw their paychecks suffer along with the company, and there was no way McGovern could put a pretty face on it.

This was a new experience for McGovern. Before forming M^2 in 1988, she was a successful consultant at Booz, Allen & Hamilton. She understood that big firms like hers often assigned their clients teams of young, fresh-faced MBAs with high IQs but little real-world business experience. Then she had an insight. She realized that many clients' needs could be better and more efficiently met through targeted advice from seasoned, independent consultants. But at the time there was no market mechanism in place to link clients with needs to consultants with skills.

That's when McGovern left her secure position to become cofounder and president of M² Consulting. As she envisioned it, M² would fill a niche between informal advice networks and expensive consulting firms. Her company would link seasoned pros who could offer targeted expertise to clients who were facing challenges beyond their core competencies.

McGovern's instincts were right. During the company's first decade, not only were prospective clients continually emerging, growing fast, and needing advice, M² was riding the wave of a significant trend toward outsourcing. The company began a ten-year run of rapid growth, adapting and expanding its capabilities to serve clients ranging from members of the *Fortune* 100 to start-ups and industries from health care to retail. It offered expertise across the entire spectrum of business needs, from finance and accounting to operations, human resources, sales and marketing, and even change management.

Along with its success, the company earned a great deal of recognition. M² was twice recognized by *Inc.* as one of America's five hundred fastest-growing private companies. It was profiled on NBC *News* and in publications like *Fast Company* and *Fortune*. M² was even featured in a study of the virtual workplace by the Harvard Business School.

And then, almost without warning, the company cratered. In 2001 M² faced a tectonic shift that nearly put it out of business. McGovern not-so-affectionately refers to it as "the tech wreck." As she recalls the pain of those two long years, she still remembers the fear and doubt brought about by events beyond her control and the frustration of not knowing what to do. Above all, she remembers the nearly paralyzing loss of nerve.

Loss of nerve is a common, if subtle, reaction when growth stalls. Every company is subject to economic upheavals, changing industry dynamics, and aggressive competition. While the timing of these tectonic events may not be predictable, their inevitability is. What is tragic is how commonly they catch companies off guard and the shattering effects they can have on the emotions of business leaders.

In general, people who succeed in business tend to be self-motivated achievers comfortable with risk and confident in their abilities. Because of their skills, these personality traits are reinforced as their companies succeed. But when hit with an unforeseen or uncontrollable tectonic event, they not only may lack the skills to cope but may even be unable to recognize what's happening.

The *Harvard Business Review* published the results of a study by the consulting firm Hay/McBer that explored the management styles of 3,871 executives from corporations around the globe. They identified six distinct management styles, each based on a different element of emotional intelligence: coercive, authoritative, affiliative, democratic, pacesetting, and coaching. Their research not only demonstrated that the best managers draw on differing research styles in different situations, it pinpointed which management style is best suited for a particular situation.[1]

When a company is adrift, Hay/McBer says, the best management style is authoritative. This is characterized by a "come-with-me" attitude as the leader demonstrates self-confidence in mobilizing people toward a clear vision or a new direction.[2] That kind of confidence can be in short supply, however, when a previously high-flying leader is hit with events beyond her control. When you've surfed the wave of growth all the way to the beach and are now being dragged back into the undertow, panic can set in. Decisions that were never questioned before now come under the microscope. Ways of doing things that have always been accepted suddenly get challenged. Confidence begins to wane. Sleep becomes more fleeting. When growth stalls, doubt can't help but creep in. And its effects are damaging in more ways than one:

- *It's confusing.* Great leaders are supposed to be firm, decisive, and sure-footed. When things go wrong, you just fix them. That is, until the problems spin beyond your control. McGovern says, "It's lonely at the top. People intellectually understand that, but when times are tough, it becomes real." She wasn't used to failing. She wasn't supposed to fail. But there she was, presiding over a failing company. She wasn't sure what to do.

- *It's discouraging.* When a company hits a speed bump, a good leader can normally overcome it using the perspective gained through years of experience. But when the road drops out from under the company, the CEO's own discouragement can be difficult to hide. As McGovern put it, "I felt like the breadwinner who all of a sudden couldn't provide for her family. When you're the founder, having to lay off half your staff is incredibly hard."

- *It's contagious.* It's one thing to struggle privately, dealing with your problems alone or with trusted advisers so your employees can take courage in your strong leadership and steady course. It's quite another when the discouragement and disillusionment hit you so hard you can't hide them. When the CEO is worried, everybody's worried. And when people worry, they start thinking about their own well-being more than that of the company. This self-interested focus, while understandable, can accelerate the company's downward spiral. Says McGovern, "If you've lost the passion, you've got to reinvigorate it somehow. You can't fake it."

- *It's paralyzing.* McGovern struggled with not only knowing what to do but finding a way to get it done. "At some level, you're just trying to make it through the quarter," she says. "It wasn't that I was creatively thinking over breakfast 'What can we do differently?' You don't have the luxury to think strategically when things are so desperate."

- *It's wearying.* Leading a company in good times is difficult enough. When the crisis hits, not only does the company place more demands on a leader's time, it occupies her thinking twenty-four hours a day. "I was just trying to figure out something new and trying to keep people motivated," says McGovern. "I wasn't so much scared as ticked off and drained. I was tired of pushing the rock up the mountain like Sisyphus."

That's why it's important for the leader of a struggling company to take a hard look in the mirror and recognize the symptoms of a loss of nerve. Understanding where you are and why you're making decisions will help you see things objectively so you can begin to take corrective action. The research we conducted on a broad cross-section of struggling companies revealed three specific symptoms that can serve as markers of a loss of nerve: fear of risk, resistance to change, and reluctance to invest.

Fear of Risk

As Marion McGovern was trying to right the ship at M^2, Congress threw it a potential lifeline by passing the Sarbanes-Oxley Act. The new law created a sea change in corporate governance that McGovern knew would cause huge headaches among thousands of prospective clients and a big opportunity for M^2. But how to tap into that opportunity? She had already cut the marketing budget to zero, and M^2 wasn't exactly swimming in free cash flow. McGovern knew she could coalesce consulting expertise around a new offering focused on Sarbanes-Oxley compliance but was fearful of launching it. "Would people really buy it if we put our stake in the ground?" she thought. "Will it work?"

Figure 6.1. Companies Somewhat or Strongly Willing to Take Creative Risks (Stalled 37%; Healthy, 58%).

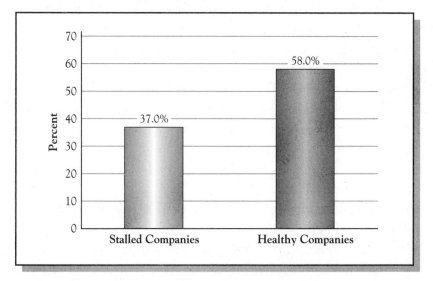

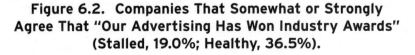

Figure 6.2. Companies That Somewhat or Strongly Agree That "Our Advertising Has Won Industry Awards" (Stalled, 19.0%; Healthy, 36.5%).

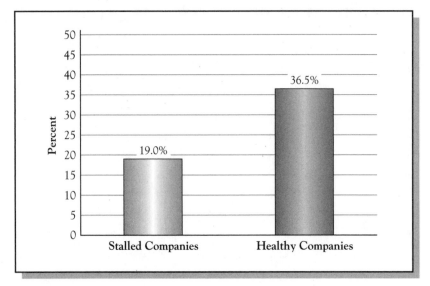

McGovern's hesitation is not unique. Stalled companies are significantly less willing to take risks. They are less likely to say they're proud of their marketing efforts. And they're less likely to create bold advertising that gets noticed in the marketplace and recognized by their peers.

Gap is one of retailing's most famous success stories. During its heyday in the 1990s, Gap became the nation's largest specialty retailer, growing its sales by more than 600 percent.[3] It was the destination of choice for baby boomers outfitting themselves for casual Friday and the weekend. Gap's unconventional CEO, Mickey Drexler, grew the company from less than $500 million in revenue in 1983 to more than $11 billion at the end of the century with a mix of street smarts and instincts.[4]

Gap's cultural impact reached its peak in 1998 with the release of its famous "Khakis Swing" television commercial in which a group of buff, beautiful young people swing-danced in their Gap khakis to Louis Prima's "Jump, Jive an' Wail." *Adweek* magazine described the spot as "hyperkinetic," a colorful adjective that also described the impact it had in the marketplace. Gap was simply the hippest brand in retail, and the company was anointed 1998's "Marketer of the Year" by *Advertising Age*.

But in 1999, Gap ran into trouble. Its same-store sales began a long and steep decline. Drexler seemed unsure of what was ailing the company, offering a variety of explanations for the slump, including contradictions like sticking with outdated styles past their prime, going with too-trendy looks, changing merchandise too quickly, or not changing styles quickly enough.[5] In 2002 Drexler moved on.

Gap's worried directors chose a new CEO, Paul Pressler, who had a successful background at Disney and a strong belief in market research. Whereas Drexler had ruled based largely on instinct and guts, Pressler put together a "consumer insights" staff that embarked on a multiyear program of research. He hired economists and statisticians to study every element of the business. After two decades of management-by-intuition, a research-based approach seemed the safe and prudent way to go. Gap used the numbers to guide its merchandise mix as Pressler cut expenses and reduced new store openings.[6]

But the designers and merchandisers who had built the Gap brand saw research not as salvation but as surrender. They began leaving the company, and after a brief turnaround, Gap continued its long and painful slide. Within five years, Pressler was gone.

Today Gap continues to languish. One analyst described its predicament this way: "You have a company that's got almost no pricing power, declining traffic, declining free cash flow, and brands that are losing relevance in the marketplace. That does not really add up to a very good situation."[7] Gap's former interim CEO, Robert Fisher (a Gap employee since 1980), said on his appointment, "Designers need to be in a position where they can think creatively. We've become too bureaucratic and overly analytical."[8] Gap's stalled growth led to a culture-killing loss of nerve, not only hampering its advertising approach but also decimating its ranks of designers and merchandisers.

It's easy, of course, to act as a "Monday morning quarterback" with respect to decisions made by M^2, Gap, and other stalled companies. What's harder is determining which risks are worth taking and which should be avoided in real time.

Myron Scholes is a former professor at Stanford, MIT, and The University of Chicago. He's also an expert on risk, having won the Nobel Prize in economics for his groundbreaking studies of the subject. About risk he says, "We all have a taste for it. In life, it would be kind of boring if there was no risk. On the other hand, if there's too much risk, too much uncertainty, too much chaos, we can't handle it either. We simultaneously want order and disorder, simultaneously want risk and quiescence."[9]

When growth stalls and the loss of nerve begins to take root, quiescence is indeed attractive. But not all risk can be avoided, so the key is to pinpoint the right risks to take. That's a guessing game for any CEO, but Scholes suggests a way of thinking that may help. He believes that companies should outsource as much "generalized risk" as possible and focus on "idiosyncratic risk"; that is, risk related directly to a company's core competency, where the company's unique knowledge has a chance to produce better-than-expected results.

Gap's core competency had always been the instincts of its designers, and managing fashion risk was the company's core competency. It made sense for Gap to outsource a variety of other risks—financial, legal, production, distribution—to companies who specialize in those arenas. But it should never have outsourced its fashion risk to its customers, which was the net effect of allowing itself to be driven by market research. Trying to minimize all risk may have been the biggest risk of all.

Resistance to Change

Fear of risk, the first warning symptom of a loss of nerve, can drastically reduce a company's flexibility and creativity. But when that fear becomes generalized into a broader fear of all kinds of change, the result can be paralysis, which often proves fatal. Hence, the second symptom you must be on the lookout for: resistance to change.

Innovation is a funny thing. Every company *says* it values innovation, but in practice many don't, especially when the heat is on. Stalled companies know they need to do something to increase the sophistication of their marketing efforts, but when loss of nerve strikes, they are often afraid of making a mistake. That can paralyze them in the present.

M^2's McGovern knows what that feels like. Years before the tech wreck, one of her board members, Robert Kriegel, had written (with David Brandt) a popular business book, *Sacred Cows Make the Best Burgers* (1997, Warner Books). McGovern distributed it to her staff, feeling confident that it represented the core culture of her company. When times got tough, she realized that she had to put what the book suggested into practice and think about her business differently. "We had to be even faster and more responsive," she told me. But that meant change, and when it came to her employees, she found plenty of sacred cows lurking within the company's halls. McGovern realized that paying lip service to iconoclasm and innovation was a lot easier than actually living by those values.

Resistance to change is a phenomenon that every stalled company struggles with, regardless of size. Intel is a $40 billion organization that owned the semiconductor market for over two decades, and no one could challenge its dominance. That is, until it was hit with a three-punch combination that would have floored a lesser company. The 1990s tech bubble burst, causing Intel's largest clients to rein in their spending. The PC market matured, slowing demand for semiconductors. And AMD, an aggressive competitor that had long toiled in Intel's shadow, rolled out new products that better met the needs of giant customers like IBM, Dell, and HP. Intel's earnings were cut in half, its stock price fell by two-thirds, and 10 percent of its workforce found itself out on the street.

Sean Maloney, Intel's executive vice president of marketing, described his feelings at the time in an interview with *Forbes:* "It was a swift kick in the gut," he said. "We were angry and disappointed in ourselves." Maloney and CEO Paul Otellini knew the company needed to change—and change fast—but it wasn't easy to do. Speaking of the employees, Maloney says, "Their whole notion of self-worth was based around bigger and faster. That aspiration needed to change to cooler, sleeker, smaller. That's a big deal."

One of the transitions Intel had to make was to develop chips that ran cooler. To make this shift, they would have to sacrifice power, something Intel had never done before. David Perlmutter, leader of the development team in Israel working on the new chips, struggled with the idea. "The company had been so successful in the 1990s, it was hard to talk about doing things differently. It was easier to be remote and question the basic religion of the company."

But after three long years of development and delays, in 2003 Intel released its Centrino chip. It became the new standard for notebook PCs and increased Intel's 2004 worldwide PC market share to an incredible 81.6 percent.[10]

Why do companies resist change, particularly when growth stalls? According to A. J. Schuler, an expert in leadership and organizational change, initially it's because the risk of change is seen as greater than the risk of standing still. He says, "Making a change requires a kind of leap of faith: you decide to move in the direction of the unknown on the promise that something will be better for you. But you have no proof."[11] And there's the rub, particularly if the company had been doing well on its previous course. Leaders who pride themselves on patience and steadfastness may be being seduced by their twin sisters, avoidance and denial.

Change is risky, and when sales are in the tank, a common response is to retreat to old habits, not realizing that they're not likely to make things better. In fact, they often make things worse.

Buick is one of GM's ever-struggling brands, selling fewer than half the number of vehicles today than it did twenty years ago.[12] The average age of people who buy Buicks is older than sixty, and according to J. D. Power and Associates, the brand is retaining less than half of them.[13] One analyst described the problem in loss-of-nerve terms: "You start to think that those older people don't like change. So you never change, because it's too risky."[14] Because

Buick is unwilling to take the necessary risk to refine its focus, it won't be able to replace its core customers as they die. Rebecca Lindland, an analyst at forecasting firm Global Insight, put it more bluntly: "The buyers who are about to be Buick buyers hate Buick."[15]

Contrast that with another GM brand, Cadillac. Imagine what it would have been like to walk into a stark, windowless conference room at GM and propose that they associate their premier brand with the long-haired, rebellious rock-and-roll of Led Zeppelin. In the seventies or eighties, you would have been thrown out in mid-sentence. But by the turn of the century, Led Zeppelin's fan base had grown up, gotten jobs, raised kids of their own, and now had significant disposable income. They had become good prospective Cadillac buyers.

GM wisely recognized the opportunity and was willing to take the risk. And it paid off. When the campaign launched, Cadillac unit volume was just over 172,000 vehicles. Five years later, it was over 225,000. And GM was able to exempt Cadillac from the profit-squeezing, zero-interest financing the company was offering on most of its brands at the time.[16]

GM's willingness to risk change with its flagship brand is the exception to the rule. Most companies wouldn't take such a bold step. Change is unnerving, but when growth stalls, it's often necessary. However, just as not all risks are worth taking, not all change is good. It can be hard to distinguish strategic changes from desperate ones. It can be difficult to differentiate between change that sharpens your company's focus and that which forsakes it.

The first step is to critically analyze the market tectonics that brought your company to its current condition. They may be purely economic, such as a recession, in which case the best solution is to resist change and ride it out as best you can. As one of our survey respondents told us, "Remember, it's a long ride. Keep a couple of spare tires in the trunk."

Even during recessionary times, however, other tectonic factors may also be at work. It's true that Kodak was hit hard by the terrorist attack on 9/11, after which leisure travel (and the picture taking that goes with it) came to a grinding halt. But that only exacerbated the changing dynamics the company faced from the rapid shift to digital imaging. Kodak's challenge was not to get out of the "memory preservation" business—that would have been a loss of focus—but to make the drastic changes required to keep the company at the forefront of its industry in a time of massive and irreversible technological transformation.

Changing dynamics are a given, and smart companies always keep one eye on how they may need to evolve. Southwest Airlines has been the most consistently profitable airline over the past two decades. But the airline's success could easily have masked a deeper-rooted need for change.

All airlines have been badly buffeted by volatile oil prices. During the early years of the twenty-first century, Southwest successfully navigated huge increases in fuel costs through a smart hedging strategy, turning steady profits while competitors lost huge sums. But the core business was struggling. Without the fuel-hedging program, Southwest would have broken even or lost money in eight of the sixteen quarters between 2003 and 2007.[17]

Gary Kelly, who developed the fuel-hedging program and subsequently became CEO of Southwest, knew that managing fuel costs, while essential, was not a growth strategy. So on his ascension to the top job, he quickly began implementing bold changes—not changes to the company's focus, but changes to how it executed against that focus.

Kelly led a successful lobbying effort to get Congress to overturn the Wright Amendment, which had restricted Southwest's ability to fly long-haul routes out of its Dallas hub. That gave Southwest many more growth options over the amendment's seven-year phaseout period. And he implemented an airport efficiency program in which, among other things, Southwest employees use stopwatches to measure the time customers wait in the check-in line. Kelly has made some daring moves, including modifying Southwest's open-seating approach, one of the airline's hallmarks. As he put it in an internal memo in early 2007, "The threat to our future is real. Now is the time to lead."[18]

Reluctance to Invest

Fear of risk and resistance to change are dangerous symptoms that can block a company from recognizing the need to adapt to changing circumstances. But the third symptom of a loss of nerve is even more insidious. Reluctance to invest can prevent a company from acting on its own best instincts, providing a rational-seeming excuse for doing nothing in a situation where dramatic, sharply focused action is the only path to recovery and renewed growth.

Geico is the most aggressive advertiser in the insurance industry. Between 2004 and 2007, the company increased its annual advertising spending by 75 percent and became the only leading player in its industry to achieve double-digit growth over that period. In a J. D. Power study, an amazing 91 percent of insurance shoppers reported they had seen or heard at least one Geico ad in the previous twelve months. The next closest competitor was State Farm at 80 percent, which has been the number one insurance carrier by market share since 1942.[19] Geico has been willing to take advertising risks, not only with its spending but with its messaging as well, using a lighthearted, fun approach in an industry traditionally dominated by serious and sappy commercials.

Contrast Geico's approach with that of Krispy Kreme. After going public in 2000, Krispy Kreme achieved double-digit same-store sales gains and seventeen consecutive quarters of growth. But in 2004, when sales went flat and profits slipped by 56 percent, Krispy Kreme cut back on marketing and slashed new-store openings. As then-CEO Scott Livengood put it, "There's no point in opening stores if we aren't able to achieve the full measure of their potential."[20] That's a loss of nerve.

Earlier I referred to a report Deloitte published entitled "Growth Companies—The World's Top 200."[21] It examined the behavior of successful companies from a broad operational perspective. Here's what the report had to say about reluctance to invest: "As sales increase, the will to grow, the commitment to growth, increasingly wanes. Signals of a lack of commitment include reduced investment in growth drivers such as R&D, marketing and capital expenditures."

Companies in fast-moving industries like technology and pharmaceuticals know better than any that R&D is their lifeblood. British drug maker GlaxoSmithKline (GSK) responded to declining revenues in 2008 by increasing its investment in research and development. CEO Andrew Witty says, "I want to ensure this company does not have periods of boom and bust." His goal is to broaden GSK's assets beyond the ten drugs that account for some 60 percent of sales.[22]

Contrast Witty's approach with that of embattled Motorola, which cut R&D jobs by 25 percent in 2008. While the struggling company justified the cuts as a way to "optimize R&D investment and focus on projects that deliver the greatest value for Motorola," it's hard to see how investing less in innovation will help Motorola compete with the likes of Cisco, Nokia, and Apple.[23]

The same is true of marketing investments, as struggling companies in our research admitted that they were less likely to fund their marketing plans sufficiently. Marketing spending varies widely

Figure 6.3. Companies That Somewhat or Strongly Disagree That "We're Funding Our Market Plan Sufficiently" (Stalled, 42%; Healthy, 19%).

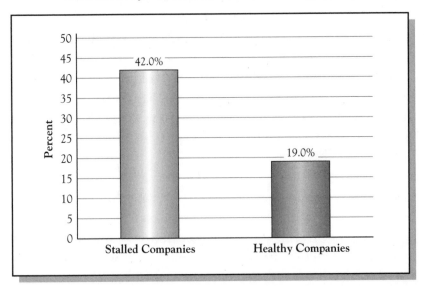

by industry, but across the study as a whole, our respondents invested an average of 4.97 percent of sales on marketing and advertising. Those in high-volume, low-margin industries like grocery stores invest a tiny fraction of their sales on marketing, whereas low-volume, high-margin companies like specialty retailers invest significantly more. Most companies fall somewhere in between.

But regardless of industry, the struggling companies in our study invested an average of nearly 8 percent less than those that remained on the growth curve. M^2 was no exception. McGovern said, "I was always scared about spending more money than I had—more scared than in the past." As a result, she cut back drastically on marketing.

This is a common, and natural, response to stalled growth. When the top line shrinks and the bottom line turns red, cutbacks need to be made somewhere. But companies often make the mistake of seeing cuts in the marketing budget as a pain-free way of saving money because they often don't involve salaries or other overhead that's more difficult to trim. But when your company's growth train is slowing down, marketing needs more fuel, not less. Looking back, McGovern would agree. "We should have been doing more brand-building," she said. "You should never stop explaining who you are and what your value proposition is."

McGovern learned the hard way that the short-term gain of cutting the marketing budget can be more than offset by the long-term problems it causes. Reflecting on her company's return to health, she said, "I probably didn't invest in marketing fast enough. In retrospect, I would have spent more dollars in marketing sooner. You can't starve your brand. The more you starve it, the longer it's going to take."

Loss of Nerve Is a Wake-Up Call

They say pain is a gift, for without it we wouldn't know when we were ill or injured. Loss of nerve can serve the same function in a struggling company. The authors of the Deloitte study say, "When a company comes out of the starting blocks like a rocket, its leaders tend to get seduced by their success. They believe they have invented a growth engine that will go on ad infinitum. The best thing that can happen to these fast-starters is a non-terminal but major problem to knock them back to reality."[24]

A loss of nerve is nothing to be ashamed about. It's common when growth stalls, even for large multinationals. Coke, recognized by *Marketing* magazine in 2001 as "Brand of the Century," has struggled with the changing dynamics of the soft drink industry.[25] That caused one analyst to describe it as having become "the quintessential, ultraconservative, risk-averse, let's-sit-on-our-hands-and-count-our-cash company."[26]

Commenting on a study on corporate growth, experts from the Wharton School at the University of Pennsylvania said, "All companies, from major multinationals to start-ups, face a common challenge: how to grow their businesses so they can boost earnings and enhance the value of their shares. Far too often, however, firms find it difficult to sustain growth because they become risk averse."[27]

Fear of risk. Resistance to change. Reluctance to invest. All natural and understandable responses to slowing growth. All a reflection of a loss of nerve. And, unfortunately, all too common. The first step in dealing with a loss of nerve is to face up to it and determine that you will not let it hobble your recovery efforts.

That's what Marion McGovern did. She persevered through two long years and returned the company to profitability. M^2 is now a $60 million organization, and McGovern's trial by fire has made her even more valuable as a consultant and corporate leader. I asked her, as she reflected on that period, what she would call a book she might write about her experience. The answer? *To Hell and Back.* When growth stalls, that's often what it feels like.

Has your risk tolerance declined? Are you afraid of change? Are you hesitant to keep investing in growth drivers like R&D and marketing? If you want to get your company back on track, first ask yourself whether you've lost your nerve. Until you come to terms with that, you can't get on with fixing things.

Have You Lost Your Nerve?

A loss of nerve can't be quantified, but it can be recognized. To how many of these questions can your management team honestly answer "yes"? If most, you are probably in a healthy risk-taking mode. If fewer than half, you are likely to have a problem.

- Do you sense you are taking as many risks as you used to?
- Do you feel as confident about your business as you did three years ago?
- Are you sleeping as well as you used to?
- Are the people who report to you confident in your leadership?
- Do you have a clear sense as to what your next strategic step should be?
- Are you unafraid of making mistakes?
- Has your advertising won any creative awards in the past three years?
- Are you honestly proud of your current marketing efforts?
- Do you instinctively think of change as a positive force?
- Are you sufficiently funding your company's marketing and R&D efforts?

7

Marketing Inconsistency

Take a quick test: See if you can name the brands associated with each of these slogans:

- "Mmm Mmm Good"
- "The Heartbeat of America"
- "Don't Leave Home Without It"
- "Fly the Friendly Skies"
- "It's the Real Thing"

If you said Campbell's Soup, Chevrolet, American Express, United Airlines, and Coca-Cola, congratulations. And chances are you did, at least if you're over the age of thirty-five. But why?

Marketing consistency, that's why. The advertising campaigns represented by these slogans were so ubiquitous in their time that they became part of our cultural fabric. You may not have even realized that none of the five slogans are in active use any longer.

Steve Pacheco is the longtime director of advertising at FedEx, a company that understands the value of consistency. He says, "People trust brands that have consistent approaches to their marketing. Especially in unsure times, people want to associate with brands that stand for something and that have staying power. If the mid-'90s dot-com rollup, and subsequent bust, taught us anything, it's that you can't build out a powerful and sustaining brand overnight. Creative consistency is of paramount importance" (interview conducted by author, April 19, 2008).

He's right. But when growth stalls, consistency often goes out the window. In fact, the struggling companies we studied were four times less likely than still-growing companies to say that their marketing message has been consistent.

Consider a tale of two beers: Miller Genuine Draft and Corona Extra. Have you ever noticed that no beer maker has ever conducted the equivalent of the "Pepsi Challenge"? Many beers taste alike (sharing the light color and flavor of "American pale lager"), and those that differ often appeal to diverse palates because of varying characteristics like malt, grain, hops, and fermentation. I've heard beer described as nutty, malty, herbal, sweet, floral, grainy, spicy, and a host of other things. With soda, however, differences in taste are not as subtle; the key to the Pepsi Challenge was Pepsi's sweeter taste (said to be more appealing to most people at first sip, even if they wouldn't like a whole can). As a result, beer marketing is largely based on imagery and brand personality. On that Miller and Corona would likely agree.

But that's about all they would agree on. According to *Advertising Age*, in eight years Miller Genuine Draft went through four

Figure 7.1. Companies That Somewhat or Strongly Disagree That "Our Marketing Message Has Been Consistent" (Stalled, 32%; Healthy, 8%).

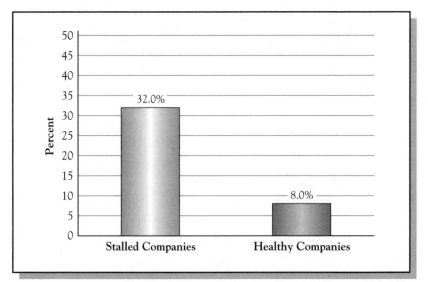

advertising agencies and almost as many campaigns, with slogans that included

- "Never Miss a Genuine Opportunity" (2001)
- "Pure MGD" (2002)
- "Keep What's Good" (2003)
- "Good Call" (2004)
- "Beer. Grown Up." (2006)
- "Experience Is Golden" (2007)

The magazine reported that Miller Genuine Draft's media spending has been inconsistent as well, swinging from a high of nearly $93 million in 2004 to a low of $15 million in 2007, and that over the course of that time the brand's market share declined from 2.6 percent to 1.5 percent.[1]

It's true that Miller Genuine Draft is in an industry that has struggled with tectonic forces including competition from low-calorie beers, changing dynamics such as the low-carbohydrate craze, and a handful of recessions. But those are all the same tectonics with which Corona Extra has had to deal, with much different results.

Corona's "Vacation in a Bottle" campaign kicked off in 1988. You've seen the television commercials: the details differ, but they all take place on a white-sand beach, with the sound of the surf and seagulls accenting the image of a refreshing bottle of Corona under a palm tree or colorful umbrella. Over the course of two decades, the brand's creative strategy remained unchanged, and sales increased every year between 1991 and 2006, even in a flat category. Economic belt-tightening resulting from the mortgage meltdown, along with an ill-timed price increase, caused a dip in Corona shipments in 2007, but independent Nielsen research shows that Corona remains the favorite import among the youngest beer drinkers, those aged twenty-one to thirty. Grupo Modelo, Corona's parent company, has no plans to change its approach.[2]

What's responsible for Corona's persistent success in the same category where Miller Genuine Draft has struggled? Industry pundits could argue about a host of factors, from Miller's longer tenure (which some say makes the brand feel tired and stale to young beer drinkers) to Corona's "cool factor" as an import. But one difference is undeniable: consistency. Corona has demonstrated it, Miller Genuine Draft has not.

Interestingly, two other brands notable for their consistent ways are also nightclub staples: Absolut Vodka and Marlboro cigarettes. Vices though they may be, you can't argue with their marketing effectiveness.

When Marlboro was launched in 1924, it was positioned as a premium-priced cigarette for women; one of its early slogans was "Mild as May." The brand name, vaguely evocative of British nobility, was selected to suggest an air of sophistication. But by midcentury the health effects of tobacco were becoming big news, and filtered cigarettes became an overnight industry staple. Philip Morris didn't have a filtered brand, so they decided to reposition Marlboro in that niche, complete with a new package design and flip-top box.

They hired Chicago-based advertising legend Leo Burnett in 1954 to work on the difficult task of evolving Marlboro's appeal from women only to a broader audience. Creator of the Jolly Green Giant, Charlie the Tuna, Tony the Tiger ("They're Gr-r-r-eat!"), and other advertising icons, Burnett was famous for creating brand personalities with human attributes, including some of the most enduring corporate images ever invented.

The next year, the Marlboro Man was born. A handsome, rugged man's man in Western duds and ten-gallon hat, he savored Marlboros against a romantic, big-sky backdrop, associating the brand with independence, adventure, and of course, masculinity. By the late 1950s, Marlboro sales had taken off, and it quickly became the number one brand.[3]

The Marlboro Man continued as one of advertising's most successful icons until the 1990s, when publicity surrounding the death from lung cancer of two former Marlboro Men put a whole new (and ironically powerful) spin on the image. The iconic image of the Marlboro Man has since been used in powerful antismoking campaigns, and former Marlboro Men have spoken out against smoking. But according to Philip Morris, Marlboro still commands an incredible 41 percent market share. Few campaigns have lasted as long or had as significant an effect.[4]

Absolut Vodka belongs in the same category. The Absolut "bottle" campaign was launched in 1979. At that time, conventional wisdom was that vodka had to come from Russia, not Sweden. To create brand awareness, Absolut began running stylish print ads that presented visual puns on the shape of the Absolut bottle, each with a unique and clever theme. Some fifteen hundred ads later, the campaign has spawned Web sites, coffee-table books, and sales growth for almost every year of its nearly three-decade run. Despite long odds against its success, Absolut has achieved 98 percent brand awareness in the United States and a strong number two position in market share, even with its premium price (and notwithstanding the fact that vodkas are basically indistinguishable from one another by taste).[5] Not only has the brand spawned more than one hundred new competitors in a once-dormant category (Grey Goose, Belvedere, Ketel One), it has revolutionized how spirits are marketed to the modern consumer.[6]

Of course, consistency is not just the purview of beer, booze, and cigarettes. Take overnight package delivery company FedEx. Steve Pacheco says, "FedEx has settled on a consistent theme, tone, style, and manner that has served us well. We have always been focused on our key attributes of reliability, trust, dependability, and innovation." Those promises were first boldly stated in FedEx's award-winning 1980s-era campaign, which promised to deliver a package "when it absolutely, positively has to be there overnight." FedEx delivered on that promise year after year, to the point where the company can now confidently say, "Don't worry, there's a FedEx for that," and "Relax, it's FedEx." Such consistency is one reason why FedEx grew more than 56 percent from 2003 to 2007.[7]

Fast-food purveyor Jack in the Box is another good example. After a disastrous *Escherichia coli* outbreak in 1993, most pundits thought the brand was dead. But the company's "Jack's Back" campaign, featuring Jack in the Box's wisecracking, ping-pong-ball-headed pitchman, was launched in 1995. The campaign resurrected the clown that sat atop Jack in the Box's drive-through speakers throughout the 1960s and 1970s, which had been blown up in a television commercial in 1980 to signal a shift toward more adult menu options. The "new" Jack, with his wry and sarcastic (some would say dark) sense of humor, is the perfect vehicle to ensure branding consistency while introducing a variety of products and promotions. Since "Jack" came back, Jack in the Box has sold more than 27 million premium items bearing his likeness and has been one of the best-performing restaurants in the fast-food industry.[8]

And then there's BMW, the world's best-selling luxury car brand.[9] Helmut Panke, BMW's now-retired chairman, once said, "We believe a company can only think in one set of terms. If you are premium, you have to focus on it."[10]

And focus they have. One of the reasons for their success is consistency in how BMW vehicles are developed and nurtured through cycles of maturity. Chris Bangle, BMW's design chief, says, "When you spend an enormous amount of money developing a new model, you don't just throw all that money out the window seven years later and do something completely different. Instead, you refine the car, you improve it, and you get your money out of it."[11]

BMW's marketing philosophy is similar. In 2000, vice president of marketing Jim McDowell said, "For 25 years we haven't changed who we are or what our tagline is. A BMW is 'the ultimate driving machine.' We've interpreted it in different ways and demonstrated it through different models, but that fundamental idea has never varied."[12]

Five years later, his boss Panke tied the company's design and marketing philosophies together. "In order to be successful, even in a tough competitive environment, you have to have a clear, authentic brand," he says. "You can't try to be something that you aren't. The ultimate driving machine has worked well in the U.S., and it will work well for new models. We are not diluting. We are sharpening and focusing. You have to be able to drive any BMW product blindfolded and feel immediately it's a BMW."[13]

That consistency of approach explains why BMW, despite not enjoying the critical mass of the world's largest automakers, is consistently one of its most profitable.

Keep in mind that consistency does not mean "sameness." It's true that BMW's tagline, "The Ultimate Driving Machine," is in its third decade, but as McDowell said, the company's advertising, like its vehicles, has evolved with the changing times. The same is true of Apple, Lexus, Nike, Harley-Davidson, and many other brands that have made consistency a hallmark. (Come to think of it, it's also true of Hallmark.)

If you were to go back and look at any of these companies' advertising, brochures, or sales kits from twenty or thirty years ago, you'd think they were as quaint as the clothing and hairstyles frozen in time in your high school yearbook. Apple's "1984" television commercial is widely regarded as the best of all time, but seeing it today isn't the same as remembering how you "saw" it on Super Bowl Sunday a quarter century ago. While its Orwellian overtones are powerful even now, the commercial itself looks dated and its special effects not so special. That said, Apple has done an amazing job maintaining the consistency of being brand Apple. The spirit of innovation that led the company to "Think Different" still fuels it today.

I've kept a few magazines in my files over the years because I wanted to hang on to a particular article or cover image. Occasionally I'll pull one out and flip through it just for fun. It's amazing how unstylish the then-new cars appear, how frumpy the fashion models look, and how silly the "advanced" technology of the day is from a current vantage point. Yet, when I first saw those ads two or three decades ago, they were as sleek, sophisticated, and impressive to me as those I see today.

Consistency in advertising is beneficial, but ads, like fashion, must keep pace with the times. Consistency of branding, however, is vital. It's true of consumer companies as well as of organizations that operate in business-to-business and even business-to-government industries.

Nitsch Engineering is a good example. The Boston-based civil engineering firm was among the pioneers of sustainable site development. Founded in 1989, Nitsch Engineering grew quickly and now serves both public and private clients in fifteen states and five foreign countries.

CEO Judith Nitsch graduated from college during the economically dismal 1970s, when jobs for new engineering grads were hard to find. She worked her way through recessions in the early eighties and again at the end of that decade in an industry closely tied to the health of the economy. When she launched her own firm, she wisely incorporated strategies for recessionary times into her business plan. Speaking of her perspective on economic downturns, she says, "It wasn't a question of if, but when. It's very hard to generate consistent growth in a cyclical industry." Nitsch Engineering hasn't wavered from its strategic plan for fifteen years.

The strategy for keeping the company healthy through good times and bad? Consistency. Nitsch Engineering continually invests in maintaining a presence at its clients' industry events and has a long-standing, lead-sharing program with noncompetitive firms that serve the same type of customers. The company invests in its reputation by submitting client projects to award shows (some of which can be quite expensive) even when margins aren't good. And Nitsch's engineers speak on sustainability whenever and wherever they can. The company has developed an educational presentation for architects and landscape architects called "Sustainable Sites," which Nitsch and her colleagues personally present several dozen times a year, every year. "Slow and steady wins the race," she told me. "We have a very consistent team that's been here a long time. We've had a plan, and we've been working the plan year after year after year, including during the down times."

Nitsch has been careful to ensure that her firm's programs offer continuing education credits for architects, to give them additional incentive to attend the workshops. When the economy slows down and architects have more time on their hands, the workshops are even more attractive and bear fruit. "Our dollar volume has actually increased during times when the market was tanking," she says.

Never had the market tanked to the extent it did in the years following 9/11. Of that period Nitsch says, "We had a number of projects that went kaput, including all work at Logan," referring to the Boston airport from which two of the ill-fated airplanes used in the terror attacks had departed. The years 2002 and 2003 were hard for the company; Nitsch herself took a 10 percent pay cut, the firm's other two board members took 5 percent reductions in salary, and staff salaries were frozen. As billable hours declined, the company's administrative-to-technical staff ratio got out of whack, but they kept layoffs to a minimum, opting instead to cut administrative staff back to a four-day workweek. They economized in every way they could but never stopped the marketing program.

In 2004 things picked up again, and by June of that year Nitsch was able not only to pay back wages but also to give bonuses and even make salary increases retroactive to when they would have been granted before the tectonic event. "We're pretty methodical," Nitsch says. "Those important—not urgent—things, we really focus on them."

Consistency Requires Discipline

Maintaining marketing consistency is difficult, even in good times. FedEx's Pacheco details a host of enemies that threaten consistency, including fear of falling behind, competition, changes in marketing leadership, and even boredom. "It's always difficult to stay the course," he says.

Competitive challenges can make consistency particularly difficult to maintain. Imagine the irritated chatter heard throughout the corridors at Coca-Cola after PepsiCo's John Sculley launched the Pepsi Challenge in 1975. The frustration (not to mention lost market share) led Coke management some ten years later to change its formula and launch New Coke, the ultimate inconsistency.

That same frustration was no doubt felt in the hallways at Microsoft each time the smart, hip Mac guy got the best of the nerdy PC (who bears more than a casual resemblance to Bill Gates) in Apple's television commercials, which is why Microsoft launched its defensive "I'm a PC" campaign in response. "Competitive hot spots," Pacheco says, "cause some on the inside to want to counter with point/counterpoint ads." Or worse, as in the case of New Coke. We all know how that ended up.

Changes in corporate leadership can also threaten the commitment to consistency. When it's "out with the old, in with the new" chief executive, operating, or marketing officer, the marketing program often gets a pink slip, too. Not only is marketing one of the easiest changes to make, it's human nature to want to create something new. Who wants to succeed using the last guy's program? The new regime can't be blamed for wanting to start with a clean slate, but the "not invented here" syndrome claims too many innocent campaigns.

And then there's simple boredom. "Our own people get tired of our ads well before the public does," says Pacheco. "You can get talked into doing oddball stuff from the agency, as well, if you're not disciplined and steadfast in your position."

Struggling companies often find that discipline and steadfastness are in short supply, often for reasons related to the other internal factors. Loss of focus is a good example. Clearly, if a company doesn't know what it is—or if it keeps changing its focus in a fruitless search for a silver bullet that will solve its problems—its marketing program is going to change right along with it.

Subway knows the importance of staying with a theme, even if it's not popular with everyone. The company has achieved more than a decade of growth on the shoulders of Jared Fogle, its slimmed-down spokesperson who has made the company's low-fat fare as famous as he is. Jared has carried commercials all by himself, partnered with professional athletes, and been relegated to cameo appearances, but he has outlasted four advertising agencies and a host of critics. Nobody would suggest that Subway's advertising is creatively brilliant (the ads eschew both high-concept approaches and high production values in favor of Jared's amateur spokesperson skills), but you can't deny its consistency and impact. Jared has enabled Subway to firmly establish in consumers' minds its point of difference from other fast-food category leaders like McDonald's, Taco Bell, and KFC.

Pier 1 Imports hasn't fared so well against the competition. By making exotic global imports accessible to the average American, Pier 1 rapidly grew to more than one thousand stores. But like any successful pioneer, it attracted the attention of companies who wanted what it had—not just niche players but Target and Walmart as well. That kind of aggressive intrusion was bound to have an effect on sales, and when growth stalled, Pier 1 dumped longtime spokeswoman Kirstie Alley in favor of designer Thom Filicia. Changing the face of the brand didn't work, and unsure of what to do next, Pier 1 halted TV advertising altogether for a full six months, including during the 2004 holiday season. That decision didn't help matters, and commenting on that year's financial results, CEO Marvin Girouard says he was "ashamed."[14]

In 2005 Pier 1 hired a new advertising agency and launched another new campaign. When that failed, the company again switched horses and tried yet another new effort in 2006.[15] Nothing worked. Although Pier 1's problems go beyond just advertising, the lack of consistency has only hurt its efforts. The company went three years without a profitable quarter,[16] and fiscal 2008 sales were down 6.9 percent.[17]

Lack of consensus is another consistency killer. When Ford kicked off a comprehensive "Drive One" marketing and advertising campaign in 2008, Jim Farley, vice president of marketing at Ford, lobbied more than four thousand dealers to give the campaign a chance. Frustrated with the company's multibillion-dollar losses, as well as with unproductive and inconsistent marketing, the dealers have to contend with Ford's consumer approval rating of only 44 percent. (Commenting on Ford's former slogan, one customer who got stuck with thousands of dollars of repairs to her Ford truck said,

"Quality must *be* job one. Saying it isn't enough."[18]) Farley admits the "Drive One" effort will need time to develop, saying it could be five years before its success can be judged. If Ford's sales don't pick up significantly before then, it's unlikely that the dealer community will give it the chance to live that long.[19]

Loss of nerve also kills continuity, as the stories of Gap and Krispy Kreme attest. Marketing is one of the easiest things to change when you're in a panic. Some companies find themselves lured by discounting ("It's too easy to fall into the discount trap" when times are tough, says Pacheco), others by cutting back their marketing investment. But consistency of spending is just as important as consistency of message.

When growth stalls, it's easy to think of marketing as an unnecessary expense, much as you might cut back investing in your retirement plan if your personal income takes a dip. But marketing results, like investment returns, are cumulative. They should be judged not only by what they deliver today but by what they will add up to tomorrow if you invest in them consistently. Great brands are built brick by brick, one touch point at a time. Each day you cut back marketing is an opportunity lost forever. You may need to conserve cash as you reposition the company for growth, but don't look at your marketing program as an easy target, especially as the media market continues to evolve.

"Fragflation"

Remember stagflation? If you lived through the seventies, you do. It's when the economy suffers both high unemployment and high inflation—a combination thought impossible by most economists until it happened. In theory, high unemployment should temper inflation, as consumers pull the reins in on spending and prices come down. But in the real world, that's not always the case.

There is a similar principle in the world of marketing I call "fragflation." That's the deadly combination of fragmentation and inflation in the media. Let me explain.

Your prospective customers simply do not have the mental bandwidth that they used to. There are more TV and radio networks vying for their attention. There are more news sources, most available twenty-four hours a day. There are virtually limitless entertainment options, both offline and online, and the Web is so large and diverse that from a practical perspective it may as well be infinite. All of that adds up to a tremendous amount of clutter in the marketplace—and thus in your prospects' minds—making it more difficult than ever for any one company's message to gain a toehold. That's the problem of fragmentation.

But there's also inflation. With the addition of each new television network, each new magazine, and each new Web site, the number of people reached by existing networks and publications continues to decline. Yet, the rates they charge for time and space don't come down. In effect, the price per customer reached keeps climbing. That's the problem of media inflation.

Combine the two, and you have fragflation, a silent, deadly, marketing-effectiveness killer. Our internal research suggests that just by standing still, implementing the same media plan it went with in the previous year, a company could be losing as much as 20 percent of its effective buying power, depending on the industry and other market characteristics. Most companies don't consciously process this thought, but the effects of fragflation are the equivalent of cutting your marketing budget by 5, 10, or 20 percent a year. If you wonder why your efforts seem to be losing impact, it's because they are.

Unfortunately, fragflation is a fact of marketing life. And it's a big reason why message consistency is vital. As media grow more expensive and less efficient, it's more difficult every day to seed any kind of identity in the marketplace. The more you can stay on point, the better it will enable you to adjust to the changing media landscape.

That's a big advantage for a company like FedEx. Pacheco says, "You need to be able to be fast and flexible with your media strategies. We never plan media further than 12 months out because we don't know what'll be out there."

I Want It *Now*

The biggest challenge to consistency, however, may be the pressure for immediate results. That's true of all companies, but especially those that are publicly traded. Bob Nardelli, who after his Home Depot experience became CEO of privatized Chrysler, was asked at an early staff meeting if the company was bankrupt. "Technically, no," Nardelli answered. "Operationally, yes. The only thing that keeps us from going into bankruptcy is the $10 billion investors entrusted with us." I doubt he would have felt free enough to be that frank if hundreds of Wall Street analysts were still breathing down his neck (or if he knew he'd be seeking a government bailout a few months later).[20]

The average tenure of a CMO, according to recruiting firm Spencer Stuart, is less than two years.[21] CEOs fare better, with the average tenure of S&P 500 company chief executives being five years. But historical trends are illuminating. In 1980, 64 percent of CEOs had been with their companies for twenty-five years or more. By 2007 this number was down to 29 percent.[22] Clearly, the level of impatience with company leadership is high and rising.

Whether recruited out of a company or forced out, leadership teams today have less time to prove themselves than did their historical counterparts. And that's dangerous. Ian Beavis, vice president of marketing at Kia Motors America, stated the problem well when he said, "If you're a CMO and you know chances are you won't be there long, you're not going to make the right decisions for the company long term."

The heat can be almost as great on smaller, privately held companies that don't have Wall Street peering over their shoulders. Pressure from investors, bankers, suppliers, and even employees, who in a competitive recruiting environment expect regular pay and benefit increases, forces company leaders to keep the growth pedal to the floor. When things start to slow down, the temptation to change marketing horses can be tremendous. Sometimes it is necessary to make a change, but it should be attempted with great caution. As Sony's general manager for corporate identity, Hikoh Okuda, put it,

"Brand equity is not something that's built in a day."[23] It may sound blindingly obvious, but if you start over, you're starting over.

Consistency Is Vital

It can be difficult for companies that once were at the top of their game to adjust to tough new marketplace dynamics. But sacrificing their long-term marketing strategy is a temptation too many give into, sometimes without even realizing it. The companies with the strongest track records do everything they can to maintain a consistent identity in the marketplace, even as the economy moves up and down, competitors come and go, and consumer tastes shift. When growth stalls, change may indeed be in order, but before you decide to dispense with your current approach, determine to address the other dynamics that may be plaguing your company from within and feeding off one another.

Are You Being Hurt by Inconsistency?

Consistency doesn't mean that you never evolve your messaging, but it does mean your brand should stay on a singular trajectory over the long haul. See how many of these questions to which you answer "yes." One or two yes answers may not suggest a problem. But if you answer affirmatively to more than a handful, you may have a consistency problem.

- Are your marketing objectives undefined or unclear?
- Are you failing to achieve your marketing objectives?
- Do you have a muddy brand positioning?
- Is your brand personality undefined or unclear?
- Have you changed campaigns more than once in the past five years?
- Have you changed advertising agencies more than once in the past five years?
- Have you had significant turnover in your internal marketing staff?
- Do you have a lot of false starts in your branding efforts?
- Are you more opportunistic than strategic in your marketing?
- If you laid out all of your ads and collateral materials together, would some of them look out of place?

8

The Vicious Cycle

If you've read this far and your company is struggling, by now you probably recognize the symptoms of a lack of consensus, a loss of focus, a loss of nerve, or inconsistency within your organization. You may, in fact, be struggling with two, three, or even all four of these issues. If so, it wouldn't be surprising.

Remember Zippo, which ran into market tectonics that caused its growth to stall? In Chapter 4 I quoted the company's chairman, George Duke, discussing the first problem, saying, "It was difficult to come to a consensus in a timely manner. It was very hard to embark on a strategy." But a lack of consensus was not the only problem with which the company struggled.

As *Inc.* highlighted in its corporate profile, Zippo also suffered from a loss of focus as it flailed about looking for a silver bullet that would solve its growth problems: "There was the ZipLight, a battery-powered flashlight in a traditional lighter casing. There were Zippo pens, belt buckles, and money clips. There was the ambitious attempt to license the Zippo name to upscale Swiss watches . . . and there was the push to expand Zippo's offerings in the collectible market." The efforts did not achieve the desired results, and the article went on to highlight the natural reaction it caused among management: "[As] such attempts failed, executives pulled back and nerves began to fray."[1] Loss of nerve was a natural side effect of Zippo's lack of consensus and loss of focus.

Zippo's experience in suffering from a multiplicity of internal challenges is not uncommon. In fact, in many ways it's the norm. When growth stalls, everything begins to break down. Confidence wanes, confusion reigns, and it can be difficult to tell which problems are cause and which are effect. A lack of consensus, a loss of focus, a loss of nerve, and marketing inconsistency tend to feed off one another in a cruel and vicious cycle, crippling efforts to turn the company around, sometimes without even being noticed. While board meetings and strategy sessions focus on the external dynamics hindering growth, the biggest enemy often lies within, creating a negative chain reaction while doing damage by stealth.

Allan Loren, former CEO of D&B (formerly known as Dun & Bradstreet), would likely agree that internal dynamics present the biggest test—and the greatest opportunity—for a struggling company.

When Loren joined D&B in 2000, the renowned information services provider was hurting. In an interview published in the *McKinsey Quarterly*, Loren described what he found when he came on board. It included a lack of strategic consensus ("We had too many decision makers and weak decision making"), a loss of focus ("The company had no direction, no strategy, and lacked the ability

Figure 8.1. The Vicious Cycle.

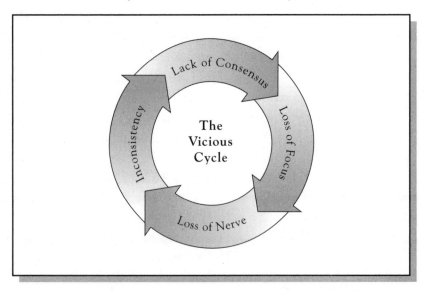

to focus"), a loss of nerve (demonstrated by the company "not investing" in the business), and inconsistency ("We had hundreds of ways of going to market, mainly because each part of the company viewed itself as separate and independent").[2]

Loren began to change the company from the inside out. "Creating a new culture was fundamental to the new strategy," he said. "We weren't trying to be all things to all people, we weren't trying to be perfect, and we weren't trying to be brilliant. It wasn't the strategy that would carry us; it was leadership, created through cultural change, what we call 'winning culture.'" Loren's approach led to a transformation of D&B and a multiyear run of double-digit earnings growth.[3]

Earnings growth is something not-for-profit organizations don't technically have to worry about. But they do need to keep revenues ahead of expenses, and they face the same struggles with the vicious cycle as their for-profit brethren when growth stalls.

The Maricopa County Community College District in Arizona is the largest community college district in the country, serving more than 200,000 students. The biggest school in the district is Mesa Community College (MCC), which, with more than 25,000 students, is larger than many universities. Ted Christensen, dean of Instruction for Learning Technology at MCC, is worried about the district's multiyear declining enrollment trend.

Christensen sees two market dynamics at work that conspire against the community colleges' offerings. The first is competition represented by the growth of surrounding universities, from the nearly 40,000-student University of Arizona in Tucson to the 60,000-student Arizona State University, with its multiple campuses in and around the community college district. The second is the incredible multiyear run of job growth in the Greater Phoenix area, which provides abundant opportunities for high school graduates requiring no higher education or external training. While that scenario is good for inexperienced job seekers—at least in the short term—it's bad for community colleges that depend on increasing enrollment to fund their operations.

What is the community college district, and MCC in particular, doing about it? Not enough, contends Christensen. And he pinpoints the number one reason why: "The problem that I see," he says, "especially in the academic world, is that it's hard to get consensus. Because we can't get consensus in some areas or it takes us a year or two to reach it, we're falling behind. We can't make decisions. That's a culture that I really think has got to change." Christensen says that the problem was not easy to spot as long as things were going well. But since enrollment began to decline, the organization has not been capable of making decisions rapidly enough.

Making matters worse is that MCC has had five different presidents in a two-year time span, including three acting presidents. "You can't blame acting people for not making major strategic decisions," says Christensen, "but it's caused major problems."

Predictably, MCC is also suffering from a loss of nerve with respect to its budgets. As a community-based organization, the district can't control its investment spending as a private company might, so budgets are being cut. That said, if there was strategic consensus, the budget cutting could be more surgical in nature, protecting (or even increasing) the budgets of the programs that are performing well and cutting back in areas that will have the least student impact. But that is not the case.

"It's across the board. Everything's being cut back," Christensen says. "It seems to me that good management would be to say, 'Let's build on those areas that we have strength in and maybe look at eliminating areas where we don't have strength or where our lead is disappearing.' But it's easier to make an across-the-board cut than it is to make decisions about what should or shouldn't get cut."

Inconsistency is also a problem facing the district. Christensen believes that the vast array of marketing materials produced by the organization is, in a word, "incongruent," with differing styles, imagery, fonts, and tone. He says it's because, as with a lot of academic institutions, the funding for marketing comes from individual programs as opposed to a centralized marketing department.

Interestingly, the one area in which Christensen believes the institution is making progress is that of focus. "It's better if you've initiated it rather than having . . . a crisis situation thrust it upon you," he says, "but now that things are tight and sort of stalling in a lot of areas, we've pulled back and said let's get back to the core of what we do here. We're teaching students—that's our top priority—and I think we've become more focused out of necessity." In that sense, the district's stalled growth is bearing good fruit, both for its current student body and those it will be around to serve in the future.

With the continued growth of the Greater Phoenix area, MCC and the community college district will probably survive long term, especially as they adapt to changing dynamics such as technology-based distance learning. Though they may have ups and downs, the need for the services the institutions provide is always there, and barriers to entry for competitors are high, giving the community college district a good opportunity to outlast its current growth stall.

That's not the case for restaurant chains, which are always endangered species. Einstein Bros.® Bagels, a three-hundred-plus unit chain with locations in twenty-seven states, almost went the way of the dinosaur a few years ago. It saved itself from extinction under the strong leadership of Paul Murphy, who became CEO just as the company was emerging from a restructuring. Yet, success—let alone survival—was not a foregone conclusion.

Murphy, who joined Einstein Bros. in 1997 as senior vice president of operations, is a classic food guy. His experience includes high-level operational roles with Steak & Ale, Bennigan's, and Boston Chicken. In 2002, he was appointed COO of Einstein Bros., and he earned the top job a year later. Of that period, he says, "Frankly, it seems to me that the minute I got there we were in trouble. The decline really started because the original business model was somewhat flawed."

Murphy describes the problem as one of inconsistency:

We had ten or eleven area developers acting independently from each other and from the company as a whole. As you traveled across the country, you'd see a different look and different products and almost a different way of doing business. Everybody delivered what their view of the brand was, and that wasn't always what the parent company thought it should be. And it certainly was not consistent from group to group. I think that was a real issue for the company . . . a lack of consistency and a lack of delivering the same brand promise to all the customers across the country.

Inconsistency in operations and branding, along with the rise of fast casual competitors and the low-carb craze (from which a bagel chain simply can not hide), led to inconsistent results. That meant that the company couldn't generate the revenue it needed to work its way through its problems. "We did not have access to capital, and it was clear we were not going to be able to produce enough cash flow to grow ourselves out of the issue," Murphy said. "I think that was partially what led to the restructuring."

But inconsistency was not the only problem. Reflecting on the other internal dynamics—a lack of consensus, a loss of focus, and a loss of nerve—Murphy said, "At that time, I think we had cracks in all three." Which among them was most challenging? "Loss of nerve, frankly. In some of our first meetings, cash really was king for us." Not only was Murphy unsure the company could continue to service its debt, he wasn't sure he would continue to be able to pay all of his employees. "A lot of what we did was out of a defensive posture," he said. "I'd been part of a highly leveraged company for some time, and I don't think you sleep quite as well."

Murphy had many sleepless nights as he worked with his team to chart a new course for Einstein Bros. While the chain had reorganized its debt to emerge from restructuring in 2003, it still wasn't growing. In 2003's year-end earnings release, Murphy unveiled his next big move: "Working with two prominent consulting firms," he said, "we are today addressing our brand position. For 2004 we are dedicated to the revitalization of our franchise brands through the appropriate reimaging of menus and the store prototype." It was a decision Murphy would later come to recognize as a distracting loss of focus.

The company announced a new name and a new concept called Einstein Bros. Cafe. A news release announcing the change proclaimed: "Moving the brand beyond the bagel, Einstein Bros. Cafe expands on the well-known Einstein Bros. Bagels artisan-baking heritage with this new concept. Einstein Bros. Cafe offers a lunch and dinner menu with a culinary focus on innovative items using the freshest and highest quality ingredients. The restaurant's new look is designed to position Einstein Bros. Cafe as a 'dine-in' choice conducive to meetings, family meals, and groups dining out together."[4]

Einstein Bros. was downplaying its bagel heritage in an effort to stay relevant in a changing competitive landscape. At the time, Murphy was quoted as saying, "When Einstein Bros. Bagels was launched, we were the leader of the quick casual pack, providing great food in a creative environment. Our success lies in our ability to recognize that quick casual diners have grown more sophisticated in their expectations. . . . We have done our homework, and while we stay true to the core tenets of what makes Einstein Bros. popular, we are very excited about what Einstein Bros. Cafe will offer."

The core concept of Einstein Bros. Cafe—besides the obvious dropping of the term "bagels" from its brand—was an upgraded menu and an environment that encouraged customer lingering. The new concept changed not only the Einstein name but also its logo, its menu, its décor—virtually everything.

While bagels were still part of the breakfast menu, Einstein Bros. added new items such as a brie and Black Forest ham baguette (served with sweet grain honey mustard, apples, and greens) and Italian chicken panini (served warm on a ciabatta with pepperoni, pesto, spinach, roasted red pepper, and provolone cheese). The cafe also offered "flavorful options to those seeking low fat and low carbohydrate selections," such as an albacore tuna salad, low-fat turkey chili, and tuna niçoise. Einstein Bros. Cafe also featured a "tossed-to-order" salad station and egg frittata sandwiches served with fresh fruit or sliced tomatoes.

Meals were served on real dishes with flatware rather than with the traditional paper plates and plastic utensils. Coffee cups gave way to ceramic coffee mugs. Karen Bebus, Einstein Bros. brand manager at the time, said, "The Einstein Bros. Cafe experience is about the food. The switch to tableware defines the quality of our food and creates a dine-in atmosphere. Guests are more inclined to relax and enjoy their meals versus taking it to go."[5] As Murphy put it, "We're not abandoning the bagel . . . we're moving beyond the bagel."[6]

Although Murphy credits the cafe as coming at a time when the company needed to be energized, it wasn't the answer to turning Einstein Bros.'s fortunes around. The cafe concept performed well in the lunch segment but caused a loss in breakfast revenue. The experiment may have succeeded as an entirely new concept, but it was too big a departure for the Einstein Bros. brand. In 2004, same-store sales were down 1.9 percent. Murphy and his team decided to keep some of the innovations developed for Einstein Bros. Cafe but return to a renewed focus on the original brand.

Speaking of the decision to pursue a more upscale identity, Murphy says, "Hindsight's always 20/20, but when I look at that decision, the conventional wisdom back then was that bagel companies or the bagel category had been turned into a commodity, so that a bagel chain could not make it on a national basis." At the time, the thousand-plus Panera Bread locations were taking the quick-service restaurant world by storm with their fresh-baked bread, made-to-order sandwiches, delicious soups and salads, and average unit sales higher than even those of McDonald's. "Conventional wisdom," Murphy says, "was that you had to move your brand beyond the bagel and seize more of a lunch opportunity and develop a broader appeal and a broader message."

That conventional wisdom was appealing in part because of the lack of consensus among the Einstein Bros. team at the time. "Was there any disagreement or unsurety? Oh, I think a lot," Murphy says. "Frankly, I think that during that time the senior team was a little bit lost in the wilderness."

But Murphy is not into shifting blame:

> I think at that point in my career as a CEO, I listened to too many people from the outside instead of listening to what my inner thoughts were. It came about because the . . . company for two or

three years had been on a downhill slide. A lot of people basically wrote us off. You know what? They probably had a reason to. Everything that we were hearing from consultants was that we needed to get beyond the bagel, we needed to be more like a Panera or something like that, we needed to have a broader reach, we needed to really emphasize lunch, or whatever.

And it's funny. When we did that, we really saw a jump in lunch. But we also saw a decline in people using us for breakfast. And the cold hard facts were that as we looked at the concept, we couldn't go back and retrofit all of our stores to put in the seats necessary to drive enough lunch business to offset the decline in breakfast.

Although the cafe concept had a fatal flaw based on the company's inability to afford the immense cost of converting all of its stores, it also provided an unanticipated benefit: affirmation of what customers truly valued the Einstein Bros. brand for. "What came out of it," said Murphy, "was that there was still very strong brand equity in Einstein Bros. Bagels. And the feedback we got about change—'we view you as bagels'—told us that we could go out there, return to it, and do a better job of executing and delivering the brand promise. The cafe was not a failure in that a lot of the elements of the upgrade to our new prototype came out of it." Those elements included a handful of the new menu items, new menu designs, and a more efficient order-taking system.

Murphy and his team refocused the company, dropped the name change, and put one foot in front of the other in an effort to improve everything from operations to marketing. "In the end, I think, being close to the business, we should have really listened to our heart and our gut and said, you know what? The cold hard facts are that we're not investing in the business, we're not doing a very good job of executing," he said.

In 2005 sales began growing again, and within two years, revenue was up 3.3 percent overall, with a 3.7 percent gain in same-store sales.[7] While still understandably concerned about the economy, competition, and continually changing industry dynamics, today Murphy is bullish on the company's prospects: "I think this restaurant group can have the best year it's ever had," he says. "But it's going to be based on its ability to not only be aggressive on the front end, but to have the right things on the back end as a backstop."

Interestingly, as Murphy reflects on what Einstein Bros. is now doing right, he talks in terms of the same internal dynamics we've already discussed:

- *Consensus:* "The company is just now to the point where the senior team is starting to work together from a consensus standpoint. In survival mode, a lot of stuff went through me. Now it's shifted. If the company is going to move quickly, departments have to communicate well together, work well together, and not wait for the CEO to be involved to make a lot of the decisions. One person can't be involved in 80 or 90 percent of the decisions of the company and, frankly, two or three years ago I was. The business acumen of the whole company is improving, and it needed to improve."

- *Focus:* "Einstein Bros. is trying to do less and do it well. You better stick with the one that brought you to the dance. No matter what anybody wants to say, the hook for the company is and always will be bagels. It can do some other things, but as it does those other things, there needs to be some aspect of a bagel involved. Einstein Bros. needs to always be mindful of that heritage and that hook and make sure that it's protected. At the beginning of the year, I put out this little manifesto to the top fourteen or fifteen people, saying this year is about leadership and their ability to remain focused."

- *Nerve:* "We were aggressively opportunistic in fixing the balance sheet. In February 2006, we did a refinance with Bear Stearns—ironically, we outlasted them—and they dropped our interest rate. Back in 2005, the company was paying anywhere from $21 to $23 million in interest a year, and now, after a public offering and paying off additional debt in June 2007, interest on the debt is only $6 to $7 million a year. That's a big change, and it allows the company to take those monies and invest them back into the business.

"Existing stores are now being upgraded and the company is seeing the results. What's exciting is not only in the first twelve months, but in the second twelve months remodeled stores have demonstrated strong growth. As the company becomes aggressive, the mind-set of its leaders really does change. They go from being defensive to saying, 'You know what? We're winning.' And when you're winning, you have a spring in your step and you're not working out of a fear of failure; you're working out of a determination to succeed."

• *Consistency:* "From a marketing standpoint, we basically started over with very simple things—blocking and tackling—like having a consistent message in-store. We just went and fixed the basics and used that as a starting point. That's really what we did. We took our marketing all the way back, just like we had in operations. In very much of a building block process, we worked on one thing at a time. Einstein Bros. isn't like the German army anymore, doing battle on a lot of different fronts for which it didn't have the resources from a human and financial standpoint."

Murphy believes he is a better leader for having navigated this growth challenge. "When I first came to the company, we were happy to make payroll. And I had to do that at a time that was maybe not as favorable to business as it was a couple of years before. I think I grew up at the right time in the sense of the needs of the company."

Having successfully navigated the minefield of stalled growth at Einstein Bros., Murphy closed the book on this chapter of his career and decided to move on to his next challenge. But he's taking with him what he's learned and understands the vital importance of avoiding the vicious internal cycle. "I see the psychological as being the biggest challenge in situations like we faced at Einstein Bros. No matter what the company or industry, you have cost pressures and other things, and you just have to deal with them to different degrees. It's keeping your people engaged and really focused that I have come to realize is the biggest issue."

Whether your organization is large or small, public or private, consumer or business-to-business, it's subject to the challenges of internal dynamics. And when one of those dynamics wedges its foot in your door, it's easy for the other three to follow behind, creating a cycle of frustration. This vicious cycle, like each of the individual internal dynamics, doesn't reveal itself with great fanfare. It simply festers, reinforcing a destructive environment out of which it can be incredibly difficult to break.

The good news, as D&B, Einstein Bros. Bagels, and a host of other companies can attest, is that it can be done.

Are You a Victim of the Vicious Cycle?

If the vicious cycle is a problem in your company, you may already know it. But it's possible that so many things are going wrong that you don't know how to gauge them. Here are a few questions you can ask yourself to get a sense of the extent of the challenge:

- Do you recognize a problem in your company with two or more of the four problematic internal dynamics: a lack of consensus, a loss of focus, a loss of nerve, or inconsistency?
- Is your corporate culture unusually dysfunctional?
- Do you have unusually high turnover?
- Are you unable to pinpoint which issue came first?
- Are you unsure which issue to address first?
- Does a discussion about one issue invariably lead to a struggle with the others?
- Do you find yourself in a loop of frustration as you consider how best to solve things?
- Have you recently introduced a reorganization that isn't working?

9

Take a Deep Breath

If your company is suffering from stalled growth, you've probably recognized in it many of the symptoms I've been describing. Hopefully, the previous chapters have given you greater insight into the problems you currently face and why they tend to reinforce and perpetuate one another. And that leads to the all-important question: Now what?

It's one thing to understand the reasons why your company is stalled on the roadside shoulder. It's another to figure out how to get it back up to speed. The following four chapters offer practical, real-world advice on how to do just that. Each chapter is designed to help you overcome one of the four destructive internal dynamics that take root when growth stalls.

Some of the principles you'll read are based on well-known fundamentals from which all companies, especially those that have stalled, have a tendency to drift. Others are new and are meant to challenge and stimulate your thinking. Follow them in sequence, and you'll have a road map by which you can create better days ahead.

That said, before you can do the right things, you need to think the right way.

Mindset Matters

When my own company's growth stalled, I spent a great deal of time feeling downcast, certain that I had done something wrong. Because we had been on such a positive upward trajectory for so long, I really thought we had figured out the special sauce that would enable us to generate consistent growth. When things slowed down, I naturally looked in the mirror and blamed it on the chef. With the benefit of hindsight, I now know that while not all my decisions were correct, the break in our company's fortunes was largely due to conditions beyond my control. Since then, I have come to understand that leader's guilt is common when growth stalls. However, that attitude is not only unhealthy and unproductive, in most cases it's just plain incorrect.

If you're in a position of leadership, you obviously have proven talents and capabilities. You've gotten to where you are through a series of smart, successful decisions. But you can't be all-seeing or all-knowing. There is no way to anticipate exactly what, when, and how tectonic forces will shake your company, nor to know which windows may crack or ceiling tiles may fall when the tremors arrive.

Planning for adversity and future challenges is an essential duty of any leader. But as the "U. S. Army Leadership" manual knowingly states, "No plan survives initial contact with the enemy."[1] In other words, stuff happens. Economies crater. Competitors innovate. Technology advances. People leave. There is simply no way you can keep tabs on every piece of information, every shift in the playing field, every risk that could threaten your organization. As long as you're using valuable brain cells stewing on what you may have done wrong, you can't fully focus your energies on getting it right.

My partners and staff are a talented bunch, and together we do good work. Occasionally we screw up, and when we do, we apologize for our mistakes, take our medicine, and set about fixing things. Still, we work in a collaborative, fast-paced industry in which problems arise literally every day through no fault of our own. Sometimes it's a printer that goofed and has to put a project back on press, delaying our promised delivery date. Sometimes it's an interactive programmer who, in fixing one bug, unwittingly creates two more. Sometimes it's a cable TV network that runs the wrong commercial or a research firm that can't get its interviews done. Sometimes critical staff members are out sick, effectively halting work on key projects.

In all these cases, I tell my people to remind themselves of a simple six-word axiom: "*Not* my fault. *Is* my problem." The principle behind this statement is that they shouldn't waste time feeling culpable because something went wrong. Sure, they may have to be the bearer of bad news, and that's no fun. And getting things turned around may in fact blow up their schedule for a day or two (or longer). I encourage them to not get angry or frustrated but instead take a more optimistic view and say to themselves, "Who better to solve this problem than me?"

You can take the same perspective. In fact, if you're going to pull your company out of its stalled-growth morass, you have to. Regardless of how circumstances came to be, you must dispense with unproductive emotions and focus on the challenge if you're going to turn your organization around.

It may not be easy. As long as your people are disengaged or divided, things are not going to get any better. Our research demonstrates that when growth stalls, management teams are not only less likely to be aligned on strategy, they are more likely to have problems with human fundamentals like mutual trust and respect. Those are essential matters, and they're not going to fix themselves.

No Heroes, Please

Some CEOs are famous for leading by dictatorial resolve or sheer force of personality. Jack Welch at General Electric, Steve Jobs at Apple, Richard Branson at Virgin, and a handful of others are so intelligent, so focused, and so charismatic, it seems they have little problem ensuring that their visions are achieved. But leaders like these are rare, and their companies will be no better off than yours once they move on. And I suspect that, if you were to ask them, each of these leaders would be the first to tell you that they can't do it all alone.

Several years ago, I had an afternoon to kill in Seattle and called on an executive at Starbucks whom I'd met at a marketing conference. She graciously offered to give me a tour of the company's corporate headquarters and spent a couple of hours with me as I peppered her with questions while we wound our way through the building.

As a student of marketing, I wanted to make the most of this opportunity to peek behind the curtain of one of the greatest brands in the world. I wanted to learn about the foundation of Starbucks' success and how the people on the inside lived and breathed the brand. I wanted to know what informed them, what drove them, what the master template was. Surely it had to be set in stone somewhere. Surely there must be "the three truths" or "the four pillars" or some sort of marble pedestal on which the Starbucks brand sat.

But I searched and searched and asked and asked and came up empty.

I don't know if I was more surprised or disappointed. Just as Dorothy discovered in her Emerald City, it all came back to the man behind the curtain. That's not a complete surprise; everybody knows Howard Schultz is the visionary behind the Starbucks brand. It's also not to say that there aren't legions of talented people at Starbucks executing his vision. But I was stunned how noninstitutionalized the internal understanding of the Starbucks brand was. It convinced me there were some tough times ahead for the company because at that time Schultz had recently stepped down from his CEO duties. Sure enough, things subsequently got rough for Starbucks and, in 2008, Schultz returned to help refocus the company and turn around its declining U.S. same-store sales.[2]

Despite their larger-than-life stature, even leaders like Schultz, Jobs, and Branson can't do it all. And they certainly can't do it forever. To once again quote Peter Drucker: "No institution can possibly survive if it needs geniuses or supermen to manage it. It must be organized in such a way as to be able to get along under a leadership composed of average human beings."[3] (Note, too, that investment genius Warren Buffett uses a similar philosophy to guide his stock picks, counseling investors to look for a company that is so good an idiot can run it, because sooner or later one will.[4])

Your people are, of course, not idiots, but I suspect that, like you and I, they are average human beings. That means they bring to the table their own strengths and weaknesses, their own ideas and opinions, and their own biases and perceptions. If you've done your recruiting job right, they also have a great deal of intelligence and motivation. What they may not have, when growth stalls, is confidence—in you, in the company, and even in themselves. Self-doubt isn't a disease that strikes only CEOs or those in the executive suite. Anybody who has been psychologically invested in your company's historical success—and its current trials—is struggling with it emotionally, no matter how well they hide their feelings.

The problem, to quote a philosopher a few thousand years older than Drucker, is that "illness strikes men when they are exposed to change" (Herodotus, 484–420 BC). Going backward is unfamiliar terrain to businesspeople who are accustomed to success. It's frightening, it's confusing, and it's decidedly unrewarding. As long as denial, doubt, and fear—and in some cases, sniping, finger-pointing, and other destructive behaviors—are wreaking havoc with your internal dynamics, you'll remain stuck in the vicious cycle.

It's easy to overreact in this situation. Although bad management apples may cause some of the harmful conduct, your first reaction should not be to lop off heads. As your company struggles, everyone on your team is trying to muddle through in their own unique way. Take a deep breath and reflect coolly on the situation before making abrupt personnel moves that may end up making matters worse. And be prepared to give grace.

Sounds a little touchy-feely, doesn't it? But it should not be a surprise. A company is not only the source of its staff's livelihoods, it also represents a considerable amount of their personal identity. If it's failing, they're failing, and their natural reaction is to act out of fear or defensiveness, which is why your corporate culture may not seem as fun and functional as it once was.

Management consulting firm Accenture has done significant research focused on "high-performing companies," those at the opposite end of the spectrum from the stalled companies we studied. Their research provides an interesting reinforcement of our work. One of their findings emphasizes the importance of what they call a company's "emotional field." Accenture's Jane Linder says, "Emotion is the silent partner behind organizational success, especially when it comes to the capacity for continuous renewal. Although executives may regard effective project management as something that demands rationality in the extreme, Accenture research has established a direct link between employees' emotional engagement and their performance."[5]

That's as true on the downside as it is on the upside. Linder explains that denial of workplace emotion doesn't make it go away but instead causes it to go underground.[6] This is the situation in which many companies find themselves when growth stalls, and it's the root of much internal conflict. Arguments over strategy and tactics abound as members of the management team cope with their emotions and view the stalled growth elephant from their individual perspectives. Even the best-intentioned people can pinball between an honest desire to right the company as a whole and their interests in protecting their own turf and budgets. Should we lower prices or stand pat? Announce layoffs or hold tight? Use cheaper ingredients or move upscale? Cut the marketing budget or invest to grow?

Because the destructive internal dynamics associated with stalled growth are psychological, the first step of the solution is psychological as well. Job one is to ensure that trust, consensus, and clarity are reestablished among your senior management team. It doesn't sound sexy, but you can't effectively address the tectonics shaking up your company, let alone the issues of loss of focus, loss of nerve, or inconsistency, without first getting everybody to the same table, literally and figuratively. It begins with a common understanding of the task at hand.

10

Set Your Sights

It's easy to argue about strategies and tactics. There are so many different ideas (and combinations of ideas) about in which direction any company should head that you can easily get stuck in analysis paralysis. It's a common problem in any sphere where complex challenges must be addressed. Just look at the national political realm: nobody on either side of the aisle likes war, pollution, or poverty, yet they vehemently disagree about what to do about them.

For the moment, however, set aside arguments about how to fix the problem, because they tend to exacerbate internal divisions. Instead, focus on where agreement is much more likely to be achieved: the solution.

Now, by "solution" I don't mean the "how" of overcoming stalled growth. I'm speaking of the "what." Think of it in terms of an algebraic equation, which may involve any number of variables but only one answer: in mathematical terms, its solution. If you're going to solve the equation, you have to start somewhere, and when growth stalls, the best place to start is by articulating exactly what the solution must be. In other words, what must success look like? We call this the "Top Box" because it's a single overarching objective to which a company must commit if it is going to emerge from stalled growth. It's the highest rung on the recovery plan, the supreme objective toward which all of the members of the management team (and by extension, every employee throughout the organization) must focus their efforts and energies.

Notice that I said "management team." It's not uncommon that a CEO will forge his or her own key objective and believe that is enough to get the company back on track. But research and experience alike demonstrate that unless the *team* that will be tasked with accomplishing that objective comes to its own conclusion about its importance, even the team members' own good intentions may derail it. This is why the act of generating consensus around the Top Box is critically important.

We practice this approach when we lead client firms through our strategic planning process. One of the first things we pursue with the senior management team is an understanding of each member's conception of what the company's key challenges are and what ultimate success will look like. Sometimes they have ideas on the tips of their tongues; other times, we have to probe by exploring their perspectives on the company's pain points. Either way, our purpose is to gain a realistic understanding of their existing mindset and the goals they see their companies needing to pursue.

Inevitably, the number of objectives we unearth exceeds the number of people we interview by a factor of at least three. If there are five members of the management team, there are fifteen or more conceptions of what the Top Box should be. If there are seven members, they may have twenty-one or more ideas. Each person has multiple ideas of what needs to be accomplished, and often they're not sure themselves how to sort them out. Most of these ideas are *not* contradictory or mutually exclusive. But they are unique, and different people, working against unique objectives—no matter how complementary they may be—are likely to end up working at cross-purposes.

Here's an example. One of our clients is a company in the tech industry run by smart people who are students of both marketing and technology. Their knowledge of our craft—and their average IQs several points above ours—keeps us on our toes at all times. Yet, they began, like all of our clients, with multiple conceptions of what their Top Box should be. Here are some of the ways individual members of the company's management team initially conceived of success:

- Generate a high level of profitability
- Be a growing company with multiple offices and development groups
- Own a brand that is the first choice in its product categories, trusted by customers and respected by competitors
- Provide long-term return on investment
- Be known for quality and excellent customer service
- Develop and attract leadership talent to achieve long-term growth
- Achieve regular citations in books, trade press, and mainstream media

These are just a handful of the objectives we were dealing with as we embarked on the development of this company's growth strategy. Contradictory? No. Mutually exclusive? Probably not. Different people on the management team simply had differing conceptions of success based on the chair in which each sat.

But what if the company had gone about pursuing all of these objectives with equal intensity? Not only would they have operated inefficiently, sooner or later they would have run into a conflict that would have affected resource allocation. This, in turn, would have caused a new round of internal dissent. What would have happened, for example, when the goal of attracting expensive leadership talent to achieve long-term growth conflicted with the desire for a high level of profitability? Or when having multiple offices and development groups hindered customer service? How would those conflicts have been resolved? Likely through either a power struggle or executive fiat, neither of which is conducive to consensus and teamwork.

Here's another example, this one from a consumer services company for whom we uncovered no fewer than thirty-seven different conceptions of the Top Box:

- Be the number one household name in our category
- Achieve consistent 15 percent same-store sales growth

- Have 8 percent more locations
- Achieve better operational compliance
- Dramatically increase market share vis-à-vis primary competitors
- Generate a measurable increase in brand awareness and differentiation

Again, all of these are worthy goals, and it's possible that they all may have been achievable in the context of a well-ordered plan. But if the development team was focused, for example, on establishing 8 percent more locations while the operations people were preoccupied with enforcing operational compliance, conflicts could easily arise.

The way to identify a single Top Box is to draw out of the team all of their proposed objectives, sort them into a logical context, and come to agreement on which goal (or which synthesis of several goals) most truly characterizes the company's highest objective. The process is not as difficult as it may sound. All that's necessary is to compare each objective with the others and identify which one is dominant and which ones are subservient.

Think about the consumer company above. If you were on its management team, which do you think would be the dominant objective: to become the number one household name in your category or to achieve consistent 15 percent same-store sales growth? Put differently, if you could only accomplish one or the other, which would you give up? Would you rather be a household name with flat sales or zoom up the growth curve in relative obscurity?

The answer is obvious: becoming a household name is subservient to achieving sales growth. Becoming a household name may indeed be one *strategy* you pursue to achieve the objective, but it is not the objective itself. The same is true of adding more locations, improving operational compliance, generating brand awareness, and even increasing market share. (It is possible to increase market share without growing, after all. Just ask Zippo how it felt to dominate the declining refillable-lighter business.) Each is important and perhaps even vital to the success of the enterprise. But only one can stand alone as the Top Box. The rest may be understood as potential strategies to accomplish the goal.

Developing the Top Box is an important and relatively straightforward exercise that solicits each team member's input about what the company needs to accomplish, provides a vehicle for careful consideration of subordinate goals in the context of the big picture, and enables the team to naturally achieve consensus away from the pressures of day-to-day decision making. It is vital, however, that whoever is facilitating the process allows honest exploration, conversation, and give-and-take. When everyone on the team comes to the conclusion together and understands how their conception of success relates to the company's as a whole, they are much more likely to embrace the result. That is a foundation of consensus on which a solid recovery plan can be built.

Simple, Singular, and Directional

What does an effective Top Box look like? It depends on where the company is in its growth cycle and sense of urgency. But the first thing to note is what a Top Box is not: it's not a corporate mission statement.

Mission statements get a lot of grief, much of it deserved. Too often they're collections of meaningless platitudes that emerge from committees with little relevance to the rank-and-file employees they're designed to serve. Occasionally, a mission statement is simple and well crafted, such as Google's mission "to organize the world's information and make it universally accessible and useful."[1] Yet, even the clearest mission statement does little more than outline a general global statement about a company's raison d'être. A Top Box, by contrast, is a specific, measurable objective with a real time frame on which a company can focus to get back on track.

For some companies, it may be necessary to achieve a critical sales volume within a brief period. For others, the Top Box may be the culmination of a long-term business development plan. And in some cases, it may even involve positioning the company to become attractive as a buyout target. Generally speaking, however, a good Top Box is characterized by three factors:

- It is simple (one sentence, with no ambiguity)
- It is singular (one objective)
- It is directional (a North Star that can guide subsequent decisions)

Given the nature of the challenges faced by stalled companies, effective Top Boxes tend to share one other common characteristic: a focus on generating growth. Here are a few real-world examples:

- For a company in a highly fragmented business-to-business industry with virtually no unaided awareness and low customer retention: generate 20 percent annual sales growth by attracting and retaining customers through the development of a focused brand identity that differentiates [the company] from the competition.
- For an undercapitalized consumer services firm that operated out of the mainstream of its competitive set: raise the awareness and understanding of [the company's] unique philosophy, approach, and capabilities to generate a 50 percent increase in revenue within eighteen months.
- For a struggling manufacturer of industrial equipment about whom competitors were spreading rumors of bankruptcy: generate ninety inquiries per month, which will enable an average annual growth rate of 24 percent, taking the company to $100 million in sales by the end of [date].
- For a state economic development agency that was in the bottom half of job creation: facilitate the creation and expansion of economic base jobs, moving [the state] upward from twenty-eighth in national rankings of job growth and achieving number one status by [date].

As you can see, each of the above examples is simple, singular, and directional, and each indirectly states the core challenge facing the organization. In none of these cases did the management team begin the process with consensus about what to do about their problems. In each of the cases, however, they were able to achieve full understanding and complete commitment to the Top Box. That set the stage, in all four cases, for a focus on how best to achieve it.

The Marketing Equation

You have to return your company to the growth mode. You have to keep your shareholders happy. You have to outpace inflation. You have to meet the ever-increasing wage-and-benefits expectations of a competitive labor market. To do all that, you have to achieve your Top Box. And the key to doing so lies in the marketing perspective.

Marketing? Yep. To once again quote Peter Drucker: "The purpose of business is to create and keep a customer."[2] Many struggling companies lose sight of this fundamental principle. Instead, they spend their energies on mergers and acquisitions, leveraged buyouts, or a host of cost-cutting measures. Each of these tactics has its place in the normal course of business, but each can also become a damaging distraction, especially when a company is struggling. Nothing is going to change unless you find a way to generate new, organic revenue.

Consider the metaphor of the equation again. If you think of your Top Box as the solution, you could, based on years of experience, try to guess how to make the business variables you're facing add up to it. In a sense, that may be what you've been doing since growth stalled. But as you know, guessing is a hit-or-miss approach, and it's as ill-advised in business as it is in mathematics. A better technique is to actually understand the fundamentals behind the equation and use them to guide you to the solution.

Mathematician Stanley Gudder said, "The essence of mathematics is not to make simple things complicated, but to make complicated things simple."[3] "But wait," you may say, "business isn't as precise as mathematics. There isn't a single formula for success that every company can follow." Of course, that's true. But just as the most complex algebraic challenges can be attacked through the application of mathematical principles, the most complicated business challenges can be solved through an understanding of marketing principles, and the marketing equation can provide the answers you need when growth stalls.

Here's the equation:

$$\text{I choose X} = \text{Top Box}$$

"I" represents the prospective customer you're trying to serve, "choose" represents the decision they're going to make, and "X" represents your brand, product, or service. A few examples will demonstrate the point.

Imagine it's just after the noon hour, and you have an appointment across town in forty-five minutes. You're hungry, and you need something to eat. But you don't have time to go to a restaurant, and the crackers you have stowed in your bottom desk drawer just aren't going to cut it today. Because you have to drive several miles to your appointment, you decide to pick up a bite of fast food along the way.

But where? As you walk through the parking garage toward your car, you mentally stake out the path you'll take to get to your appointment, visualizing the colorful and familiar fast-food signs that you've passed dozens of times. "There's a McDonald's up at the corner," you think to yourself, "but I don't really want all those calories. And behind that in the strip center there's a Subway, but I don't want to have to stop and get out of my car. Plus they usually have a long line at this time of day, and I don't have time for that." You keep thinking. "Taco Bell has those burritos that are easy to eat on the road, but I'd have to turn left across three lanes of traffic, and that's such a hassle." You're just about out of options when it hits you. "I know: Wendy's. It's a little bit out of the way, but if I change my route, it won't slow me down much. Plus they have a really fast drive-thru and that new pita bread thing. Perfect." Wendy's gets your business, you get a satisfying (and not too unhealthy) lunch, and you arrive at your meeting on time. Problem solved.

What I just described is the kind of purchase decision that millions of people make each day. It's what keeps all those fast-food purveyors in business. You no doubt made a similar decision yourself today; perhaps it didn't involve fast food, but it involved some kind of eating occasion, whether it was where to meet a client for breakfast, whether to work through lunch, or what to have for dinner. We call these "low-involvement decisions" because they happen so frequently that we're good at them. I daresay that in the case of the fast-food decision above, you wouldn't even consciously realize you're going through a decision process; it all happens within a matter of seconds, it isn't difficult, and the solution won't change your life. But—here's the important part—after all was said and done, your equation was complete: "I choose X," and this time "X" was Wendy's.

Let's go to the other end of the spectrum, to a high-involvement decision process: buying a car. We've all gone through the painful process of car shopping. As exciting as it is to slide into the supple leather seat of your shiny new vehicle, getting to the point of decision can be a struggle. It may be a weeks-long process, during which you'll read every ad you can find (at least among the vehicles in your consideration set), spend hours online, seek out the opinion of friends, confer with your banker, and possibly even approach total strangers ("Hey, how do you like your _____?"). You may also have to spend time with a person you'd not normally choose to hang out with, depending on which salesperson's turn it is when you arrive on the lot. You'll test-drive the cars, compare gas mileage and resale values, ask about safety ratings, and conduct the all-important cupholder comparison. In short, you'll devote significant time, resources, and brainpower to deciding how best to spend your twenty, thirty, forty (or more) thousand dollars.

Eventually, one morning, as the brochures, the printouts from *Consumer Reports*, and the makeshift spreadsheet you designed to help you sort things out cover your breakfast table, you'll turn to your spouse and say (for example), "Honey, let's go with the Audi." The process lasted much longer than your decision about where to get a bite to eat on the run, it was much more difficult, and you were probably acutely aware of the steps you were taking to narrow the search. But in the end, it came down to the same marketing equation: "I choose X." This time, "X" was Audi.

One more example, this time from the business-to-business world. Imagine you're a mechanical engineer working at a cereal manufacturing company. The company is building a new plant, and your task is to figure out a way to move tons of cornflakes from the ovens to the packaging line. You know that a mechanical process won't work (cornflakes are fragile things that can't be shoveled to and fro), so you know you need to specify, put to bid, purchase, and oversee the installation of a sophisticated pneumatic (air) conveying system.

You already know of a couple of companies that specialize in pneumatic conveying based on previous installations: Azo and Pfening. And there's another that you remember reading about in a case study in *Powder Bulk Solids* magazine: MAC Equipment. You have three viable competitors to whom you can bid the project.

After the detailed work of initial specification has been done, you contact each of the companies to gauge their level of fit and interest. After significant screening, you're satisfied that any of the three companies could handle the project, so you issue a Request For Proposal (RFP) to solicit formal bids.

When the bids come back, you and a team of six people, including the vice president of manufacturing, the COO, the CFO, and two longtime line workers, review the RFPs in detail, scoring them based on a predetermined system, discussing the merits and missing parts of each, and considering their timelines and financing terms. You may even go back and forth a few times with one or more of the bidders to clarify answers to some of your team's questions.

When all is said and done, one of the three companies is ruled out because its price is simply out of whack. But the two that remain seem to have similar capabilities; one is a little cheaper, but the other can promise installation and testing more quickly. The team deems either one acceptable and turns to you to make the final decision. What do you do? Taking in all of the information, rehashing all of the research in your head, considering all of the input from your team, and (secretly) trusting a hunch you had from the beginning, you say, "I choose MAC." (Full disclosure: MAC is a client of my firm. Yes, this particular example had a predetermined outcome.) The marketing equation again rules the day.

"I choose X" is simply the way the world of buying and selling works. I choose which restaurant to patronize, which car to buy, which equipment to specify. I choose which designer's clothing to wear, which shoes to work out in, and which thirst quencher to drink. I choose which law firm to defend me, which accountant to protect me, and which physician to treat me. I choose which university to attend, which charity to donate to, which neighborhood to live in. I choose where to spend my entertainment dollars, where to invest my retirement funds, and where to keep my checking account. In a free economy, I choose X, and I do so every day, both for my own needs and for those of my company. So do you.

The marketing equation is at work all around us, all the time. It doesn't matter how simple or complex the decision is. It doesn't matter how seldom or how often the decision is made. It doesn't matter how much the product or service costs, how many people have input, or whether it's being purchased for a small family or a global corporation. In every purchase decision, the equation comes down to one key point of inflection where the ultimate decision maker says, "I choose X."

That's the marketing equation, and if understood and applied properly, it will enable your company to win and keep customers, whether you're Wendy's, Audi, or MAC Equipment, a Fortune 500 company or an independent dry cleaner.

Is the equation limited to organizations facing stalled growth? No. MAC Equipment, for one, has been back on the growth track for years. We have simply found that struggling companies are more likely to have kinks in their equations or are unaware of the marketing equation entirely.

And there are differences, of course, in every company's equation. Wendy's needs customers to choose in its favor over three hundred million times per year. Audi, by comparison, would be thrilled with one million positive customer decisions. And MAC Equipment, relatively speaking, needs only a handful of prospective clients whose sophisticated and complex needs lead them to choose the company. But in principle, each and every company's assignment is the same: achieve the Top Box by getting enough current and prospective customers to say, "I choose X."

Speaking of which, while a few MAC customers may coincidentally drive an Audi and eat at Wendy's, these companies—like your company—each target a unique customer profile. That's where any company tackling the marketing equation must begin.

11

Find Your Target

Instead of arguing about how to fix the business—the *how*—beginning with the Top Box enables you to build a foundation of consensus around the *what*: an overarching objective that will rally the team and set a marker for success. Quantifying the Top Box, and coming to agreement on its importance, is a vital first step.

But it's still not time to focus on the *how*. Consensus is a fragile thing, and if you start trying to fix things too quickly, you'll end up right where you began, unsure about which strategies and tactics to pursue. There is still more foundation to be laid. And the marketing equation begins with neither *what* nor *how*. It begins with *who*.

Start with the "I"

In 2001 ANC Rental Corporation (parent company of National and Alamo) was struggling through Chapter 11 bankruptcy in the hotly competitive rental car industry. National had traditionally been a business-focused brand, facing stiff rivalry from Hertz, Avis, and other large players, whereas Alamo had built its reputation by serving the leisure market.

In an effort to create efficiencies that would bolster the bottom line, ANC decided to combine the operations of its brands at airports that both National and Alamo served. In a way, this made sense. Both brands had to bear the financial burden of supporting on-site employees, counter space, shuttle buses, and car fleets, all within a stone's throw of each other. By combining their operations, ANC could save a great deal of money.

There was just one problem. Both National's and Alamo's customers hated the idea. National's business travelers did not appreciate, among other things, sharing the shuttle bus with sniveling children, and Alamo's leisure travelers were confused about why people wearing a National logo were handling their reservations. ANC's concession to the bottom line generated confusion—and a host of complaints—from its customers. Within two years, new owner Vanguard Car Rental USA undid the change.[1]

ANC management had failed to appreciate the first principle underlying the marketing equation: people are different. At first glance, it may seem that everyone who rents a car has basically the same needs, and to some extent they do. But people rent cars for a variety of reasons, and a variety of motivations, perceptions, attitudes, and need states drive their decisions. I think, for example, of my own purchase behavior; sometimes I want (and can afford) the convenience of a business-focused brand like Hertz (the #1 Club Gold® rocks), and other times I go to Dollar because I want to save a buck. Failing to recognize this principle, ANC erred.

It's an error many companies make. They either try to be too many things to too many people, or they lose sight altogether of who it is they need to please. The result is a fuzzy marketing focus. That's why we preach that to solve the marketing equation ("I choose X"), you have to start with the "I."

It's a truism in business that you can't be all things to all people, and although nobody would argue with that, in practice companies tend to forget it as they chase new business. However, it's vital for any company, especially one that is struggling, to understand how best to define the "I" in its marketing equation. As we're fond of saying, "It doesn't matter what we think. All that matters is what *they* think." This is another step in the vital internal consensus-building process because it helps each member of the team set aside his or her personal biases and preconceptions and focus on what prospective customers think and feel.

There are limitless ways to define the "I." It may be partially based on gender, for example. Wharton researchers published a study called "Men Buy, Women Shop" that highlighted fundamental differences between how men and women tend to engage the retail environment. Basically, the study found that men hunt and women gather. Men want to find what they need and get out, while women enjoy the shopping experience itself. I am not sure we needed research to figure that out, but it's an interesting confirmation of what some would dismiss as a sexist stereotype. And it suggests specific issues that retailers (among others) need to think about in their efforts to attract specific kinds of customers. For example, the number one problem women cite when shopping is finding sales help when it's needed, whereas men cite parking as their number one concern.[2]

In other cases, age is an important factor. One of my favorite annual reports is the "Mindset List," published every August by Wisconsin's Beloit College. The purpose of the list is to highlight how very differently incoming college freshmen view the world compared with their forebears. Some highlights from the list for the class of 2011:

- They have never "rolled down" a car window
- They have grown up with bottled water
- Nelson Mandela has always been free and a force in South Africa
- U2 has always been more than a spy plane
- Stadiums, rock tours, and sporting events have always had corporate names
- American rock groups have always appeared in Moscow
- Commercial product placements have been the norm in films and on TV
- Fox has always been a major network
- Thanks to MySpace and Facebook, autobiography can happen in real time
- They learned about JFK from Oliver Stone and Malcolm X from Spike Lee

- Tiananmen Square is a 2008 Olympics venue, not the scene of a massacre
- They're always texting 1 n other
- They never saw Johnny Carson live on television
- "Chavez" has nothing to do with iceberg lettuce and everything to do with oil
- The World Wide Web has been an online tool since they were born
- Burma has always been Myanmar
- Food packaging has always included nutritional labeling
- What Berlin wall?

Imagine how different the world must look to an eighteen-year-old with this background from the way it looks to her parents. Or to you. Obviously, defining the "I" can have crucial implications for the ways you reach out to potential customers.

Typically, effective target insight profiles go beyond demographics to also incorporate lifestyle considerations. In the late 1990s, Roper Starch Worldwide interviewed thirty-five thousand consumers in dozens of countries and identified six distinct "value groups" that they claim define consumers worldwide. They included "Strivers," who are preoccupied with material things; "Devouts," who lean on traditional values; "Altruists," who care about social issues; "Intimates," who are very people-oriented; "Fun Seekers," the hedonist crowd; and "Creatives," who are into technology and all things new.[3]

Whether these broadly defined categories are valuable to any individual marketer is arguable, but they do highlight the point that people are different and that these differences play an important role in shaping purchase decisions.

Audi has explored the lifestyle characteristics of its buyers by creating a test based on twenty-seven either-or questions that help customers determine what kind of drivers they are. Questions probe the importance of everything from styling to the size of the trunk, from safety to the sound of the engine, and from fuel efficiency to navigation systems. Based on customers' answers to those questions, Audi places them in one of eight different categories: Sporty, Discerning, Comfort-Minded, Pragmatic, Purist, Distinguished, Art-of-Living, and Individualist.[4] Although the test may not be scientific, it reflects the fact that different drivers have differing needs and will respond to products and services differently because of them.

There are even life-stage segmentations. Chicago-based Leo Burnett did a study on motherhood and identified four different archetypes:

- June Cleaver: The Sequel Mothers, who tend to be highly educated women who believe in the traditional role of stay-at-home moms
- Tug-of-War Mothers, who share similar beliefs as the June Cleavers but are forced to work and as a result are filled with guilt and stress
- Strong Shoulders Mothers, who are younger, single, and have a positive outlook despite their lower incomes
- Mothers of Invention, who also work outside the home but have help with their kids from their husbands and have a balanced, happy home life

In a story about how these different moms respond differently to advertising, *American Demographics* told the tale of an AT&T ad in which a working mother left her messy home behind, taking her kids to the beach with cell phone in tow. While Strong Shoulders Mothers and Mothers of Invention thought the ad was charming, that opinion wasn't shared by the June Cleaver and Tug-of-War moms, who were put off by the thought of leaving a messy house uncleaned.[5]

The lesson is clear: as Harvard Business School professor and strategy expert Michael Porter says, "Deciding which target group of customers, varieties, and needs the company should serve is fundamental to developing a strategy."[6]

This is a critical shortfall that plagues most companies experiencing stalled growth. When we conducted our first study in 2003 among former members of the Inc. 500, we asked them to agree or disagree with a battery of statements on a five-point scale. We found that the companies that had stumbled were less likely to agree with the statement, "We know our customers' attitudes, perceptions, and desires intimately," and were more likely to agree with the statement, "We still haven't entirely figured out our target audience."

Bain & Company's Zook found similar results. "In a recent series of business seminars I held for management teams," Zook says, "the participants took an online survey. Though nearly all came from well-regarded companies, fewer than 25 percent agreed with the simple statement, 'We understand our customers.' In a 2004 Bain survey, we asked respondents to identify the most important capabilities their companies could acquire to trigger a new wave of growth. 'Capabilities to understand our core customers more deeply' topped the list."[7]

Our 2008 study of a cross-section of U.S. companies again confirmed the point. Stalled companies were nearly three times as likely to admit that they didn't know their customers well and more than twice as likely to report that they hadn't yet figured out their target audience. If you're going to be successful in achieving your Top Box, you have to find a way to identify and intimately understand your "I."

Real-World Examples

Many of the most notable companies that have experienced stalled growth did so because they lost their focus on their target customers, whereas companies that keep a well-defined customer in mind generally keep growing. Let's look at a few examples.

Walmart targets "people who live paycheck to paycheck."[8] That simple statement implies a host of demographic, lifestyle, behavioral, attitudinal, and need-state characteristics that define Walmart's core customer. Meeting that customer's needs has historically

Figure 11.1. Companies That Somewhat or Strongly Agree That "We Still Haven't Entirely Figured Out Our Target Audience" (Stalled, 31%; Healthy, 14%).

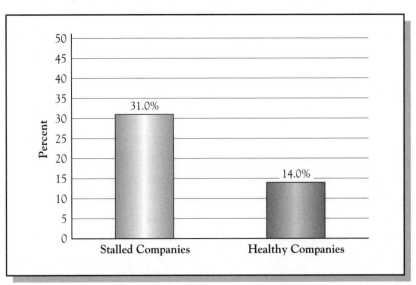

defined everything Walmart has done, from its real estate decisions to its store layout to its famous cost-management discipline.

It's also why it was such a mistake for the company to try to target a more upscale consumer (as discussed in Chapter 5). It's not that Walmart captures purchases only from people who live paycheck to paycheck; plenty of people with higher incomes shop there. But those who are more well-off shop at Walmart because they understand that the brand exists to make its core customers' limited budgets go farther, not to make them fashion-forward. Thus, they visit Walmart only when price, not style, is the key issue. (That is why Target's strategy is so smart. The cachet Target has attached to its brand is like a hard turtle shell that Walmart—arguably the fiercest competitor on the planet—can't crack without ceasing to be Walmart. Brilliant.)

Contrast Walmart's temporary loss of focus with the success of Mountain Dew. Named after a slang term for moonshine, Mountain Dew was originally positioned using cartoon hillbillies as a hook. ("Yahoo! Mountain Dew!") For years, it languished as an also-ran in a category filled with stiff competition. But in 1993, the brand began focusing on a clear target audience, which it calls "Dew Dudes": active, free-spirited young men who live life to the fullest and seek a refreshing blast of energy from their chosen soft drink. In 1995 Mountain Dew sponsored the first-ever X Games, and in 2005 the company produced *First Descent*, a movie about the snowboarding revolution. Tactics like these would have been inconceivable had Mountain Dew tried to appeal to everybody.

Having found its "I," Mountain Dew grew to become the number four soft drink by volume, still trailing Coke, Pepsi, and Diet Coke but ahead of many popular brands including Diet Pepsi, Sprite, and Dr Pepper. By focusing on its core target drinkers, Mountain Dew could offer a compelling suite of benefits designed with their needs in mind. People who don't fit the core audience can and do still buy the product (I've been known to sip a Mountain Dew in midafternoon to keep me going some days when I've been burning the candle at both ends) because they understand the product's strong appeal.

The BMW auto brand has its own strong appeal, focusing on people who "love to drive." Everything about the cars, from styling details to tire specifications to the sound of the engines—not to mention BMW's advertising—is oriented toward that customer profile. Mini Cooper, BMW's sister brand, is "for people who like to giggle when they drive," according to *Fortune* magazine, which also said, "You don't so much drive the Mini as strap it on."[9] And Lexus keeps an entirely different "I" in mind. Denny Clements, general manager of Toyota's Lexus Group, says that Lexus focuses on people to whom time is most important. Everything Lexus does, from design to features to service, is based on that focus.[10]

The principle of understanding your "I" goes beyond the products and services we typically think of as being the subject of buying decisions. Tom Brokaw, the iconic newsman who carried the NBC *Nightly News* to the top of the ratings for a decade, wrote the best-selling 1998 book, *The Greatest Generation* (Random House).

The book celebrates the heroism, bravery, and selfless contributions of the World War II generation that saved the world from Nazism and Fascism and ultimately defeated Communism. Yet the book also served a marketing purpose for Brokaw's employer, NBC. Andrew Lack, the president of NBC *News* from 1993 to 2001, intentionally oriented the NBC *Nightly News* toward an older demographic, often running features about health, nutrition, and other topics of interest to the Medicare crowd. Said one producer, "Andy attributes our success to having targeted older viewers, to having understood that that's who's watching our show."[11] Undoubtedly, Brokaw was motivated to write the book by his sincere interest in and admiration for the older Americans he profiled. But writing a paean to your target customers is a good way to reinforce their loyalty, which meant that *The Greatest Generation* provided a marketing boost for NBC *News* as well.

Fox *News* followed a similar line of thinking, albeit with a different way of defining its "I." Within six short years of the network's 1996 launch, its ratings had surpassed those of cable news pioneer CNN. Fox *News* succeeded by targeting a conservative audience that feels underserved by what it perceives as the generally liberal media. The network's founder, chairman, and CEO Roger Ailes says, "We know the audience has reasonable doubts about government, media, and life in general. We don't mind reflecting that. . . . If you want to call us populist, then there is a streak of that." Call it populist, call it conservative, call it whatever you want, but Fox *News* found a creative way to define its target and went after it with a vengeance. "I had a clear vision of what I needed to do strategically to [grow the audience], and never wavered," says Ailes.[12]

Vera Wang, the iconic fashion designer, has put her vision to the test by creating a line of clothing for discount department store Kohl's. Although Wang is known for her expensive bridal gowns and high-end fashion (evening wear priced as high as $2,800), Wang's dresses at Kohl's start at just $68. She thinks she can serve both ends of the pricing spectrum, based on how she defines her "I": "It is always the same woman," Wang says. "It is a woman who is quite confident and independent and also loves a bit of art, some unique detail, an element of surprise, even if it is a twist of a sleeve. It is about an attitude. It is about a woman who is active. She loves her life. Even if she is wearing something quite precious, she doesn't wear it in a precious way." Wang is betting that her target market's similarities in attitudes transcend their differences in pocketbooks.[13] Whether she is trying to stretch her "I" a little further than the customers are willing to go is something only time will tell.

How to Find Your "I"

There are many different variables that go into defining a core target. Sometimes demographics play a significant role (acne medication, home pregnancy tests), and sometimes they don't. Sometimes lifestyle is a major consideration, such as with video rentals or recreational vehicles. Sometimes it's behavioral (capital investments tend to involve committees, and corporations tend to replace their computers more frequently than consumers). Sometimes it's need-based (many purchase decisions are made during the back-to-school season or tied to holidays). And always—*always*—attitudes and perceptions are involved. Usually your "I" will be a function of some combination of the above.

The *Wall Street Journal* used to run a small feature called "Me & My Car." The feature always highlighted one vehicle, along with a profile of its typical driver. Lincoln LS buyers, for example, tended to be people in their fifties who were interested in wine, the stock market, casino gambling, and foreign travel. By contrast, the Jeep Grand Cherokee was purchased by people in their forties who spent their time jogging, snow skiing, and playing tennis.

A few years back, *Brill's Content* magazine published in its "Ticker" section an interesting comparison of statistics from the Book Industry Study Group and Coca-Cola: the average American purchased four books per year, but the average drinker of Diet Coke purchased seven books per year.[14] That bit of information alone tells you something that distinguishes Diet Coke drinkers from, for example, "Dew Dudes." ("Read a book? No way, man!")

The key to identifying your "I" is to do your homework. One of the tenets of Procter & Gamble's corporate principles is to "develop superior understanding of consumers and their needs."[15] But developing that "superior understanding" isn't always easy. Customers often don't realize the broad mix of attitudes, perceptions, wants, and needs that drive their purchase decisions, and even when they do, they are loathe to part with too much personal information just so a corporation can develop a detailed profile of them.

This means that an indirect approach is often more effective than a direct approach. Hans Straberg is CEO of Electrolux, a once-struggling company that he was able to turn around. His advice is, "Start with consumers and understand what their latent needs are, and what problems they experience. That doesn't mean you go and ask them, 'What are your latent needs?' or 'What problems do you experience?' You need to observe and find out by different means, and then put the puzzle together yourself to discover what people really want."[16]

Kenichi Ohmae, a University of California, Los Angeles, professor and McKinsey & Company veteran who cofounded the firm's strategic management practice, tells the story of how one appliance company set out to develop a new coffee percolator. Ohmae says, "Executives were asking, 'Should it be a General Electric–type machine? Should it be the drip-type of the kind Philips makes? Larger? Smaller?' I urged them to ask a different question: 'Why do people drink coffee?' The answer came back—good taste. After further research, the company found that this 'good taste' had a few critical components: water quality, coffee-grain distribution, time elapsed between grinding and brewing. Certain things mattered more than others. That got the company thinking differently about the percolator's essential features."[17]

Companies can use any number of advanced research techniques to plumb the hidden depths of their target audience's minds. The important thing is not to try to take a shortcut around this step or accept at face value what traditional market research may be telling you. I wholeheartedly agree with Robert Passikoff, president of Brand Keys and adjunct associate professor at New York University, when he says, "If you wish to avoid the mistakes of the past, you have to conduct research that reveals what people think, not what they say they think. To do this, you must slip behind their unconscious defenses with an indirect method that tells more about them than their alleged 'intentions.'"[18]

This is an area in which business-to-business marketers may have an advantage over their consumer marketing counterparts. Because the decisions business-to-business customers make tend to be complex, they typically engage more deeply with the companies with which they do business. That makes them easier to get to know.

You May Not Know Them, But They Know You

As the above suggests, the key to understanding your "I" may be hiding right under your nose: your current best customers. Jim Safka led Match.com to becoming the largest subscription-based dating site in the United States. To find the "I" for Match.com, Safka went to the data. He found that people older than fifty who visited the site were more likely to pay the subscription fee to communicate with other members (as opposed to just scrolling through the listings). Based on that insight, he defined his "I" as daters aged fifty-plus, reoriented the site to better meet their needs, and drove substantial increases in revenue and profit.[19]

Safka's success at Match.com got him the assignment of running sister company Ask.com, the fifth-ranked search engine with a paltry 2.2 percent market share. Not surprisingly, Safka took a similar approach to this new challenge. "The first step," he said, "is figuring out who uses Ask today and what they use it for. We have to be the first place some audience goes to."[20] Safka discovered that Ask.com has historically done well among a core group of women who use the site to ask full-sentence questions about lifestyle issues like health and entertainment, as opposed to conducting single-word or phrase-based searches. As he did at Match.com, Safka is reorienting the entire Ask.com operation to better serve those customers.[21] He faces long odds in the competition against the likes of

Google, Yahoo!, and MSN. But he's approaching the challenge in the right way.

Safka understands an often-overlooked principle of marketing: the best research is looking at the real world. Think about it. Despite your current woes, if you've been in business for any length of time, you're obviously hitting the mark for someone. Your customers have filtered all of the available rational and emotional cues about prices, product features, service dimensions, competitive options, and value propositions and have chosen you. They probably have your company's appeal figured out better than you ever could. Begin with them, and you'll have a big head start.

That's what Burger King did. In response to a question seeking the key to the company's turnaround efforts, Burger King CEO John Chidsey gave a straightforward answer. He didn't say it was the company's innovative "barbell" pricing strategy, featuring products at both the low and high end of the pricing spectrum. Nor did he credit the execution of his franchisees, which would have been politically expedient. "Most importantly," he said, "it was finding who our target customer was, figuring out who was the superfan and not wasting our time trying to be all things to all people."[22]

That's a battle-tested strategy in line with the advice of Harvard's Porter: "A small percentage of varieties or customers may well account for most of a company's sales and especially its profits," he says. "The challenge, then, is to refocus on the unique core and realign the company's activities with it. Customers and product varieties at the periphery can be sold or allowed through inattention or price increases to fade away." Porter believes that within well-established companies, there is a "core of uniqueness." He says one way to identify it is to ask the question, "Which of our customers are the most satisfied?"[23]

Broaden your understanding of the "I" by examining closely your best customers. Describe them as best you can across the six major dimensions of demographics, lifestyle, behavior, attitudes, perceptions, and wants or needs. Plumb your internal data. Conduct market research. Talk to customers in their plants or in your stores. Observe them in their homes or offices. Examine how they work and where they play. Develop a target insight profile so crisp and so detailed that everybody on your team will embrace it and say, "This is who we're trying to serve. Everything we do should be to meet their needs." Identifying the "I" that will deliver your Top Box will provide your nascent recovery efforts with focus, direction, and another crucial building block of consensus.

Yeah, But . . .

How do we know if our "I" will include enough prospective customers to achieve our Top Box?

You obviously can't achieve success by targeting a single individual, the ultimate narrow niche (unless, perhaps, your goal is to sell an investment to Warren Buffett or technology to Bill Gates). But you can't get there by targeting the whole world either. The trick is to find a niche that's big enough to achieve your goals but small enough to ensure relevance. In Wendy's case, the "I" has to be broad enough that it can generate those three hundred million purchase decisions per year. Audi, on the other hand, can focus a bit more narrowly because the company needs only a million transactions (albeit pricey ones) per year. And MAC Equipment can be even more selective in how it defines the "I." Sizing the niche can be easily incorporated into the scoping process, based both on company needs and market characteristics.

That said, most companies err on the "too big" side when trying to define their "I." Chances are that if you identify a target insight profile correctly based on what you know about your customers, a whole lot more of them are out there who have yet to be introduced to you—that is, unless you've spent so many dollars on marketing that you've achieved 100 percent awareness. Unlikely.

There's real power in the principle that the more narrowly you define your target, the more intense your brand's appeal can be. That's what Bob Lutz demonstrated when he took the reigns at struggling Chrysler in the early 1990s. His goal was to quit worrying about whether Chrysler was on everybody's consideration list and start concentrating on making cars that would be the first choice of a smaller segment of buyers. On his watch, Chrysler developed the Concorde and PT Cruiser, the redesigned Dodge Ram pickup, the Jeep Grand Cherokee, and the wildly impractical but head-turning Dodge Viper. Said Lutz, "The Viper gave us the forward momentum we desperately needed, both internally and externally with the financial community, the automobile magazines, and all of those constituencies that create the psychological climate in which your company either prospers or it doesn't."[24] His strategy resulted in record profits for the automaker in the mid-1990s.[25]

Still, there are times when a company's historical target is too small to sustain continued growth. Nike is a case in point. Here's how Scott Bedbury, who directed Nike's advertising from 1987 to 1994, described the company's predicament:

> At times in the mid- to late-'80s, our business was more than 90 per-cent young males. We knew we had to grow to include women, if for no other reason than to defend against Reebok and L.A. Gear. It seemed like a contradiction to us: How can you be the most inter-esting, dynamic brand for males 15–24, and be equally relevant to their moms and aunts? Traditional marketing people said we were crazy to try to do both.
>
> We found communications platforms that would bridge the gap. The 'Just Do It' campaign is a great example. It spoke about self-empowerment rather than something prescriptive such as being like Michael Jordan.[26]

Nike approached its growth challenge not by changing its target but by better understanding it. The company had previously thought that because men were so dominant among their customer base, there was some sort of causal relationship there. But correlation and causality are two different things. Nike figured out that its customers were not driven so much by performance as by the empowerment the brand provided to achieve their sports or fitness goals, however they defined them. Beyond gender differences, different types of athletes all have unique needs that can be met by the variety of Nike products. But they share a similar mindset, which is the basis for Nike's appeal. The company chose to focus on what its broader customer base had in common rather than on their differences.

What If We Have More Than One Target?

If you think you have more than one target, the first thing I'd do is challenge that assumption. I mentioned earlier the customer survey that identified eight unique types of Audi drivers. Should the company pursue all eight as mutually exclusive targets? That would be highly impractical. At a tactical level, there are things they can do to match each to the proper product, but they are still all Audi customers. Unless Audi wants to occupy only one of those niches— or develop seven more brands—it must base its appeal on common attitudes, perceptions, need states, or other dimensions that cut across all eight types. And it can be done, as Nike proved by overcoming its initial belief that men and women were mutually exclusive.

Motel 6 discovered this principle, and the result was one of the most successful and long-running advertising efforts in history. The Richards Group, the Dallas-based agency that developed Motel 6's famous "We'll leave the light on for you" campaign, describes the target this way: "Motel 6 guests can be segmented into three distinct groups: seniors, vacationing families, and self-paying business travelers." That appears to be a threefold target, all with different characteristics, needs, and wants. By looking deeper into the psyches of the Motel 6 customers, however, the company discovered something around which it was able to build a singular focus. Despite their differences, Motel 6 customers all had a self-image of being frugal, which, according to the agency, "represents the common denominator that predicts their behavior regardless of age, income, traveling purpose or any of a hundred other things that make each guest different."[27] Based on that realization, down-home radio personality Tom Bodette was able to relate to all types of Motel 6 customers.

If you really do have different targets, however, a different approach is required. Under these circumstances, you have to serve each "I" under the banner of a different brand. That's what big packaged goods marketers like Procter & Gamble, Nestlé, and Unilever do with their dozens and dozens of product lines.

It's also the strategy Toyota chose in 2002, after learning that nearly two-thirds of sixteen- to twenty-four-year-olds considered its brand "stodgy." Toyota had worked hard to earn its place as a dependable, trusted friend to the baby boom generation, but its success with that "I" caused it to be perceived as out of touch with younger buyers. Instead of the brand trying to be all things to all people, Toyota wisely developed Scion, a new nameplate to meet the needs of the "I" for whom the parent brand was not working.

Launched in 2003, Scion was crafted to be "a listening post to what's desired by young buyers," said Don Esmond, a senior vice president at Toyota Motor Sales U.S.A.[28] And it worked. Scion achieved an average owners' age of thirty-six (a figure that may have been overstated because some parents help their kids with the purchase of their cars). That compares with an average age for Toyota buyers of forty-nine and Lexus of fifty-three. It's even younger than the average age of buyers of supposedly hipper brands like VW and Honda, a statistic that bodes well for Scion's long-term future.[29] To top it off, some 75 percent of Scion owners were new to the Toyota family.[30] That's good news because it means that the new Scion brand isn't cannibalizing customers who would have been shopping for a Toyota anyway.

Halfway There

Once you have a Top Box on which the key members of your team agree and a clearly defined target insight profile—an "I"—against which your efforts can be directed, you're well on your way to solving the marketing equation. Now you can focus your energies on rekindling growth by better meeting your customers needs, and in the process unleash a whole new level of internal energy.

12

Sharpen Your Arrow

There's nothing like a clear objective and a well-defined target to center the mind. The task now becomes one of sharpening the arrow with which you intend to hit the bull's-eye as you focus on the "choose" part of the marketing equation.

Of course, the degree to which the arrow will fly straight and true is a function not only of its aerodynamic properties but also of the steadiness with which the bow is held. Steadiness comes from continually keeping in mind the "I" axiom: it doesn't matter what we think; all that matters is what they think. As you focus your brand while relentlessly keeping your target prospect in mind, you will naturally build consensus and confidence—even excitement—among your colleagues and employees about successfully rejoining the battle.

The "B" Word

First off, a definition is in order. You may have noticed I used the term "brand" in the last sentence, something I will be doing throughout the next two chapters. It's important to make clear that when I do, I'm not referring to some fuzzy concept out of the marketing department. I'm not talking about your company's logo or slogan. I'm referring to the meaning in the marketplace created through each and every function of your enterprise. Let me explain in a little more detail.

Nothing happens without a transaction. Until someone makes a decision to exchange their hard-earned dollars for your product or service, all of your efforts are academic. And transactions are won based on the unique combination of features, costs, convenience, performance, quality, and imagery that your company's products, services, and marketing messages offer to your target prospects. Any decision that affects one or more of those factors either increases or decreases perceived value. In that sense, there is not a single function performed by your company or its proxies that does not have an impact on the meaning of your brand.

Let me give you a few examples of how your brand is affected by decisions made outside the marketing department:

- When the head of manufacturing changes the specs on a key production component and a resulting malfunction shuts down the assembly line, customers are forced to adjust to maddening delivery delays.
- When administration streamlines internal efficiency by installing an automated telephone answering system, customers in need of assistance are required to navigate a complex and exasperating command tree.
- When the CFO recommends a sales-staff layoff to meet earnings targets, prospective customers must cope with frustrating gaps in service.
- When product development subtly trims package (and thus portion) sizes to protect margins without raising prices, loyal customers feel suckered when they run out of product sooner than expected.

As Harvard's Michael Porter puts it, "Overall advantage or disadvantage results from all of a company's activities, not only a few."[1] Everything that affects the "choose" part of the marketing equation is branding, properly defined. Decisions about every aspect of your operation, from raw materials, to pricing, to packaging, to staffing, to quality control, to advertising, must be consistent with the brand identity to which your "I" will respond. And the more that identity can set you apart from the competition, the better.

Distinctiveness Is "Job #1"

In a noisy, competitive marketplace, the worst thing your brand can be is indistinct. Some 90 percent of the thirty thousand brands launched each year fail,[2] many because they are simply yawners—too undifferentiated to offer a meaningful enhancement in value over current options.

That's why, in our research, companies that had stalled were much less likely to agree with the statements, "It's easy for prospects to tell us apart from other companies like us," and "our prospects understand our point of differentiation." They also reported having more difficulty enhancing the loyalty of existing customers. These are all problems that wouldn't surprise Porter. "Too often," he says, "efforts to grow blur uniqueness, create compromises, reduce fit, and ultimately undermine competitive advantage."[3]

Figure 12.1. Companies That Somewhat or Strongly Agree That "Our Prospects Understand Our Point of Differentiation" (Stalled, 43.0%; Healthy, 70.5%).

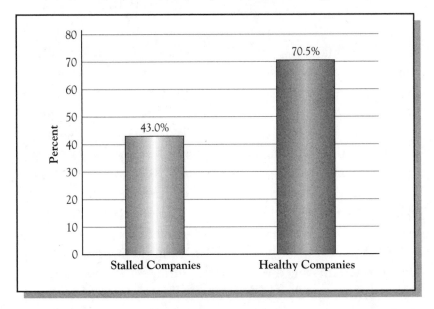

When hit with unfavorable market tectonics, a formula that may once have been successful begins to show signs of erosion. By following the marketing equation, however, you can find a way to make your brand one that again stands for something meaningful and relevant to both external customers and internal constituents.

Why is brand distinctiveness important? Because of the way people make buying decisions. Think about the marketing equation again: "I choose X." Before making that choice, your prospective customer is in a state of indecision. She knows she has a need, and in many cases she has an awareness of a handful of brands that may be able to meet that need, but she doesn't know which represents her best option. McDonald's or Wendy's? Lexus or Audi? Azo or MAC Equipment? She is, in a word, uncertain. That's why I believe an excellent definition of branding is simply "the art of reducing uncertainty."

I realize that definition doesn't sound sexy, and it certainly isn't found in any textbook, but it puts into stark relief the task facing your team. When your prospective customers embark on a buying decision, they are immediately faced with uncertainty; the first brand that reduces their uncertainty to zero gets the nod: "I choose X."

The best way to do that, for any given customer profile, is to stand out as uniquely capable of solving their problem. Jack Welch, the legendary former CEO of GE, said it as succinctly as you might expect for a man of his reputation: "Try desperately to make products and services distinctive, and customers stick to you like glue."[4]

The problem is, being distinctive is not easy. It takes nerve. It involves sacrifice. It requires a willingness to leave business on the table. It means giving up one thing to focus on another. To quote Porter again: "The essence of strategy is choosing what not to do."[5] I also appreciate the colorful analogy David C. Baker of management consulting firm ReCourses, Inc. used to describe the process of creating a distinctive brand: "Down on the farm, branding means clearly differentiating one cow from all the rest. It's not something that the cow enjoys, which is why each one has to be wrestled to the ground before its perfectly good flesh is scarred with hot metal."[6]

Hopefully, the process won't be as painful in your organization. But when growth stalls, it is vital that you make your brand mean something distinctive and compelling to the "I" on whom you are depending to achieve your Top Box.

Positioning and Trust

A great deal has been written about positioning since Al Ries and Jack Trout wrote the book on the topic more than two decades ago (*Positioning: The Battle for Your Mind*, 1981, McGraw-Hill). In fact, if you read the description of their original work at Amazon.com, you'll see that more than one hundred other books cite it. But positioning is not really a difficult concept: at root, it's simply that which makes your brand distinctively different.

Our research found that struggling companies have either lost their distinctive positioning or never had it in the first place, merely hitching their wagon to an already-growing market and hoping that will be good enough for lasting success. Sometimes companies want to avoid making a commitment to a market position so that they don't have to pass on any revenue opportunity. As Baker says, "A position is one place. It might be a big place, or a strangely shaped place, but it is a place. Brands should not be like appliqué tattoos handed out at parties and removed later to avoid questions in the elevator."[7]

The failure to appreciate this, in practice if not in theory, is why stalled companies are more than twice as likely as their healthier counterparts to lack a focused niche, and more than three times as likely to lack clearly defined positioning. As our research proves, distinctive positioning is vital to long-term growth.

The key to reducing prospective customer uncertainty lies in building trust: trust that your brand is the solution to the customer's problem or need. But there is more than one kind of trust you need

Figure 12.2. Companies That Somewhat or Strongly Disagree That "We Have a Clearly Defined Brand Positioning" (Stalled, 27%; Healthy, 8%).

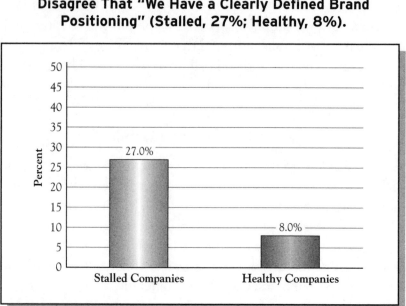

to think about. Most unfocused companies rely exclusively on relationship trust, when a whole other form of trust that's available to them goes neglected: specialty trust.

Relationship trust is the basis of all word-of-mouth marketing. When we need a doctor, an attorney, a new car, a new information-technology director, or a pneumatic conveying system, we often turn first to friends and colleagues for advice. If they can recommend a company, professional, product, or service, we place a high degree of trust in their word based on the relationship we share.

Relationship trust is the best kind of trust because it's based on personal experience. But until you earn that experience, it's difficult to build relationship trust. That's where specialty trust steps in.

Specialty trust makes the difference when customers have little or no experience with the purchase occasion (finding a surgeon, leasing a warehouse), have not made the purchase in some time (buying a car or television, remodeling a restaurant), or have a limited understanding of competing options (cell phones, MP3 players, digital video recorders). Typically, they either have no one to guide them based on relationship trust, or the purchase is too significant to base on relationship trust alone.

Specialty trust is built on a truism that we all accept, even if we don't realize it: if a brand can prosper doing nothing but _____ , it must be good at it.

Tylenol is the nonaspirin pain reliever—not necessarily the one to take for all pain relief (although the folks at McNeil wouldn't mind if you did), but the best-known, leading choice when you don't want aspirin. On the other hand, when you need an over-the-counter medicine that will mask your symptoms and knock you out for the night, it's hard to beat Nyquil. And if you just plain have a headache and want quick, topical relief, you might try HeadOn ("Apply directly to the forehead!"). Specialty trust is the reason HeadOn can prosper despite having the most headache-inducing commercials on television. (Perhaps it's a plot to inspire more purchases.)

Specialty trust, then, involves focusing on one purpose and doing that exceptionally well. In time, you and your product or service will become known for that specialty and associated with it in the minds of customers—positioning with a vengeance.

Many companies that have boasted long track records of success have a high degree of specialty trust. Need a running shoe that comes in adjustable widths? New Balance is your best bet. An IT company that specializes in health care? Cerner's the one. Enterprise software for the legal industry? Try ProLaw. A $350 loan to put a low-income, hard-to-qualify "micro-entrepreneur" into the manicure business? Acción has locations in economically disadvantaged areas all over the country. By virtue of their specialization, these brands earn enough trust right out of the gate to at least get their prospective customers looking at them.

The above examples demonstrate an important point about positioning, well stated by Ameriprise Financial's Glen Salow: "If you can't explain it to your mother or grandmother, don't do it."[8] Genuinely distinctive brands are not complicated. True, the average businessperson may not know or care what "pre-seed-stage venture capital" is, but if you're an entrepreneur who needs help getting your tech startup going, the term will become meaningful, and Verge Fund, the first pre-seed-stage venture capital firm, will be there to help.

That's why behemoths like Citi, "today's pre-eminent financial services company," with four major segments including (according to the Citigroup corporate Web site) "Consumer Banking, Global Cards, Institutional Clients Group and Global Wealth Management," tend sooner or later to collapse in on themselves. Their brands become so big and unwieldy that they no longer mean anything.[9]

Older organizations like Citi that have grown and diversified to the point where they are sprawling and ill defined exemplify this problem. But Yahoo! is a surprisingly young company to have neglected the need for distinctiveness. At the 2008 All Things Digital Conference, Yahoo!'s founder Jerry Yang was asked to define his company's business. His answer was somewhat rambling: "We want you to start your day with Yahoo!. That is home-page, that is mail, that is search, that is mobile. That is an incredibly powerful position that happens to be a position that we occupied for a lot of our history. That's our consumer goal, dream, aspiration." Company president Sue Decker then interjected, "It's a little bit of a change because we still do hundreds of things, but we're really focusing on those four areas."

Obviously, neither of them had explained Yahoo!'s business model to their grandmothers lately. Decker went on: "Without looking too much to the past, as a company we have made a few mistakes. We started as a place that people went to the Web to find what they're looking for. We were really close in those early years to the users. Over time, as we got bigger, we started organizing around products, around mail, and around search and around finance and sports. What was lost [was] the core focus around the key ecosystem—which is the user, the advertiser and the publisher and the developers. What Jerry and I have been trying to do in the last year is rewire the company." Reports from the conference suggested that those in the audience left scratching their heads.[10]

Thomas Friedman, *New York Times* columnist and author of the best-selling book, *The World Is Flat* (2005, Farrar, Straus and Giroux), says, "There is nothing wrong with complicated ideas, but if you want to convey a complicated thought to a mass audience, you have to first condense it into something digestible and believable. Once you grab someone's attention, you can pour in the details."[11] He may have been referring to political events and global economic trends, but the principle holds true in branding as well.

No doubt there are many things about your products or services that you want people to know. But it's a lot to ask of a prospective customer to allow you to educate them about your brand. It may help to think of your company as if it were a handsomely decorated home. It's something you are proud of, and you would like to invite people to come in so they can look around, be impressed, and spend some time enjoying your hospitality. Your positioning represents the door to that home, the point of entry through which people must choose to pass. If they can't find the door, or if it looks uninviting for some reason, they'll never even make it across your threshold.

The "I" Has It

You may have realized by now that your company is stalled simply because you've drifted from the historical distinctiveness of your brand. If that's the case, your task is to prune away the distractions and get your brand back to being what it was and still could be.

In other cases, you may wonder how viable your historical brand positioning is for the future. You may suspect that you need to take an entirely fresh look at your core competencies to determine how best they can create specialty trust. The good news is there's a straightforward way to go about making those decisions. The analysis may be complex, but the approach isn't. In fact, it's a lot like dating.

(To my women readers: Please forgive me, but for this metaphor I have to use a man's perspective. I'm sure its application won't escape you.)

Guys, think back to your college days when the cute coed on campus caught your eye. After observing her for several weeks, you decided on your Top Box. You'd like to spend some time with her—a great deal of time, perhaps, and possibly even the rest of your life. (I know, I'm getting ahead of myself, but I'm a romantic at heart.)

What did you do first? You found out all you could about her, talking to people she knows, noticing her favorite brand of soft drink, keeping an eye out for her around campus, even trying to catch a glimpse of what she doodled on her notebook cover. Before you risked humiliation, you wanted to learn everything you possibly could about her. This was getting to know your "I," and we covered this element of the marketing equation in the previous chapter.

Your next task was to evaluate how well you lined up with what she was looking for and determine what you needed to do to be even more attractive. The better you did that, the easier it was for you to muster up enough nerve to ask her out. If you could leverage relationship trust by having a mutual friend introduce you, by all means you did. If not, you had to find a way to develop specialty trust.

Perhaps you discovered that you had a lot in common and all you had to do is comb your hair, brush your teeth, and find a way to get noticed. In other cases, you may have needed to do more: lose some weight, take tennis lessons, get your grades up, or actually read the book you discovered was her favorite. The point is, once you understood your "I," you did what you could to ensure a good fit. That's what positioning is all about.

Of course, in business, as in romance, you have to be genuine. You could try to fake the fit on the first date, but if you were to do so, she would soon discover you were a phony. On the other hand, if there were characteristics you genuinely possessed on which you could begin to build a relationship—if you could discover a match between your genuine self and hers—the odds of success were pretty good.

As in the mysterious world of love and romance, in the business world it's rare that prospects will tell you exactly what they want.

But it does happen. Asked to explain the popular appeal of the Saturn auto mark shortly after the brand had been successfully launched, ad man Hal Riney said, "There's nothing about these cars that isn't a direct answer to what we heard people asking for."[12] Similarly, Enterprise Rent-A-Car plainly states that "it was our customers who originally led us into the neighborhood rental car business; they needed replacement vehicles while their leased vehicles were being repaired."[13]

In other cases, you may have to probe a little bit to understand where your distinctive appeal can best be leveraged. Take milk, a great example of a product once suffering from stalled growth due to commoditization (literally), changing perceptions of health and nutrition, and intense competition from soft drinks, bottled water, and substitutes such as soy milk. The now-famous "Got Milk?" campaign resuscitated milk's appeal, and while the creative execution was terrific, it arose as the result of a positioning breakthrough. Here's how Jeff Goodby, co-chairman of Goodby Silverstein & Partners, the ad agency that developed the campaign, described the epiphany:

> If we had started with the idea of milk as a glass of milk you drink alone, we would have ended up addressing the health benefits or the nostalgia of milk. Exactly as had been done in previous campaigns. Exactly wrong. We looked for the truth about milk. We asked people to go without milk for 2 weeks. 'Sure, no problem,' they said. They came back and told us how hard it was. What else goes with cereal? What are you going to do with a fresh-baked chocolate chip cookie? We arrived at the truth: Milk is never just milk. It is always _____ and milk. Milk as accompaniment. After that, everything fell into place.[14]

In still other cases, you have to go with your gut. As someone once said, "Nobody ever asked for a microwave oven." If companies relied exclusively on research rather than instinct there would be no Starbucks, no Amazon.com, no Costco, and no personal computers.

Know your target well, and you will greatly increase the odds that your gut will be correct.

Generating Options

One common hindrance from which companies suffer in evaluating their identities is a lack of imagination. While it's self-evident that there are a variety of possible customer targets depending on how they are defined, developing a wide variety of strategic positioning options can be more challenging.

We have developed a mechanism for identifying dozens of potential positioning options in a rapid, prolific, and comprehensive manner. We call it the "Some Strategy" approach because it's based on the observation that just about any well-defined brand in the marketplace can be categorized into one of five "some-based" groupings: Someone, Something, Somewhere, Sometime, or Somehow.

Here's how it works:

Someone: This is when a company bases its identity not so much on a distinctive feature or benefit of its product or service but on one or more unique characteristics of its target audience. This is the strategy successfully pursued by Mountain Dew with its focus on "Dew Dudes" and by NBC *News* with its wooing of the "Greatest Generation." It's also how ESPN launched its sports magazine in the face of its dominant competitor, *Sports Illustrated.* John Skipper,

Figure 12.3. Some Strategy.

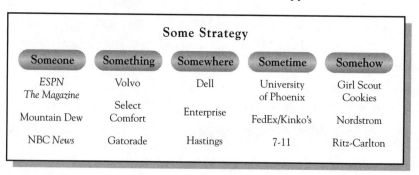

Some Strategy				
Someone	**Something**	**Somewhere**	**Sometime**	**Somehow**
ESPN The Magazine	Volvo	Dell	University of Phoenix	Girl Scout Cookies
Mountain Dew	Select Comfort	Enterprise	FedEx/Kinko's	Nordstrom
NBC News	Gatorade	Hastings	7-11	Ritz-Carlton

founding general manager of *ESPN The Magazine* said of *SI*, "The magazine that had dominated the market for years and years and years and years had gotten older. The median age of the reader was older. They weren't reaching the younger audience, the 18- to 34-year-olds. And there was an important brand name, ESPN, that meant more to [young men] than any other sports brand."[15]

ESPN went after this Someone with a vengeance. It's not so much that the people and events *ESPN The Magazine* covers are poles apart from what *Sports Illustrated* features (although there are some differences), it's that the material is presented in a way that is different and that reflects its younger reader. Peruse a copy of each, and you'll see what I mean, from differences in font size to page layout to the tone in which the articles are written.

Something: A Something strategy is used by companies in an attempt to dominate a particular category benefit. Examples include Volvo and safety, Select Comfort beds and adjustability, Gatorade sports drink and performance. It's important to note that an effective Something strategy should not be based on an attribute (which is often easily matched), but on a benefit, and it is incumbent on the company to continually innovate to maintain leadership in that benefit.

What's the difference? The best example may be the Model T Ford. It's rare to see one today, but back in the early twentieth century, Ford cranked out sixteen million of them. In the Model T's heyday, there was no such thing as power steering, speedometers, rearview mirrors, seat belts, radios, heaters, air conditioners, or even an automatic starter (imagine hand-cranking your car today). Compare that with the last car you bought, which probably came with all of the above and possibly even an iPod dock, rearview camera, and satellite-based navigation system. New bells and whistles are great, but notice how yesterday's exclusive attribute is today's standard feature. That's why no car company can succeed for long based on one or even a few attractive gadgets or options.

Instead, a company that seeks long-term success needs to focus on benefits that it can claim as its own. That's why Gatorade, for example, created the Gatorade Sports Science Institute to "enhance the performance and well-being of athletes."[16] Its scientists poke, prod, and analyze athletes in myriad ways to better understand how nutrition, exercise, and the environment all affect athletic performance and recovery. If there's an advance to be made in the realm of nutritional performance enhancement, it's a good bet that Gatorade will make it. That's the Something they're determined to own, as opposed to an attribute of the drink like a certain level of electrolytes or a particular flavor. And that's how they protect their nearly 80 percent category share.[17]

Somewhere: A Somewhere strategy is built by leveraging a distribution method. Dell didn't grow from a college kid's hobby to one of the world's largest computer makers through technological innovations or by building a better machine; it did so by mastering the direct-sales channel and wringing all unnecessary inventory and selling costs out of the retail price. Similarly, Enterprise became the number one rental car company by focusing on "neighborhood rentals" while all of its competitors fought over airport traffic.

Hastings is a retailer of multimedia entertainment (books, music, videos, and games) that offers huge selection in superstores averaging twenty thousand square feet in size. If you haven't heard of the company, it may be because you live in a big city; Hastings's growth strategy has been to build in small- to medium-sized markets where there's less competition. This Somewhere strategy has enabled the company to grow to more than 150 stores. Similarly, K-BOB's Steakhouses are scattered throughout small towns in the western United States, with the company's focus being to "carve a niche as one of the nicer places to eat in small communities of less than 30,000."[18]

Sometime: A Sometime strategy is used when speed or convenience is highly relevant to the purchase decision. The University of Phoenix became the largest private university in the United States using this strategy, tailoring its locations, semesters, and class times to make them convenient for busy working professionals. Is the education received at the University of Phoenix as good as what a traditional university could offer? I don't know, but at the University of Phoenix you can earn a degree without upending your life. That's a powerful benefit.

There were plenty of shipping options before Federal Express was launched, but none that could guarantee delivery of a package "when it absolutely, positively has to be there overnight." Oddly enough, Kinko's, now a subsidiary of FedEx, built its own valuable franchise based on a different Sometime strategy. When I was in college, Kinko's was the only copy center open twenty-four hours (and it was right across the street from campus). Throughout my career, when I've had to finish my written thoughts on the plane the night before a meeting, Kinko's has saved my bacon by helping me update my presentation or print my handouts at the last minute. And just a dozen years ago, when we launched our firm, I spent many a late night at Kinko's, my "office away from home." That's why FedEx's acquisition of Kinko's is one merger that makes sense: it smartly leverages the common and compelling positioning on which both companies have been built.

Somehow: Organizations that use the Somehow strategy understand that success may be less about the product or service than how that product or service is delivered. The single best example of this is Girl Scout Cookies. Sure, the cookies taste good, but boy, are they pricey. And yes, having them brought to your door is convenient, although it often requires a several-week wait. The reason you buy Girl Scout Cookies is how they're sold: who wants to say no to a cute little wide-eyed nine-year-old with a ponytail? It's the perfect form of manipula . . . er, salesmanship.

Upscale retailer Nordstrom is another good example, with its legendary tales of above-and-beyond customer service. Another is Ritz-Carlton ("Ladies and gentlemen serving ladies and gentlemen," as the internal motto goes). In fact, Ritz-Carlton is renowned for how it continually improves its Somehow strategy to stay ahead of the curve. It took them nearly a decade to complete a major initiative to reduce employee turnover (from nearly 100 percent a year to around 25 percent), but imagine the impact it had on training and customer service. And the company has a deep-seated understanding that, when it comes to service, even the little things matter, such as reducing customer-reported lightbulb outages (trimmed from 500 per 10,000 rooms to 1 per 10,000) and offering personal storage for repeat clients in between stays.[19]

The value of the Some Strategy approach lies in its ability to spawn dozens of potential positioning ideas that can then be screened and evaluated in whatever detail is necessary to test their potency (or lack thereof) and their applicability to a particular company or industry. I often do an exercise when I speak to college classes in which I give each student just five minutes to develop a new business concept for the quick-lube oil-change industry using this approach (quick-lube itself being a Sometime strategy). They've come up with a number of different ideas: for example, a nonintimidating, mother-friendly oil change offering toys, a clean and inviting waiting room, and age-appropriate snacks and games for kids in tow (a Someone strategy); a twenty-four-hour oil-change outlet designed to serve people who work the late shift (Sometime); and an on-site, "we come to you" oil-change service that can take care of your car in the driveway of your home or the parking lot at work (Somewhere). I have since actually seen some of the ideas they've developed implemented in the marketplace. There are innovative thinkers everywhere.

Typically, when we use the Some Strategy method for exploring positioning options for our clients, we develop six to twelve different options under each category. That gives us a total of thirty to sixty possibilities that can be evaluated for how well they'll lead our "I" to choose our "X." Not all of them survive under the hot lights of detailed analysis, but they give us a fertile place to start our thinking.

Making It Stick

Ideas in hand, it still may be difficult to determine which positioning strategy will be the best option for developing specialty trust among your target audience. At this stage, your team should evaluate each possibility based on how well it scores on five positioning tests.

First, *relevance*. If you're not relevant to your target market, you might as well be invisible. That's why this is requirement number one. Altoids is "the curiously strong mint," a legitimate and compelling positioning for a prospective customer who has bad breath. A more complex company, Procter & Gamble, has identified multiple points of relevance (using multiple brands, each targeted to different "I" profiles) in a single category, detergents. Those points of relevance include superior cleaning (Tide), fragrance (Gain), color protection (Cheer), and stain fighting (ERA).

The tricky thing about relevance is that it's continually evolving as the needs, wants, and desires of your target audience evolve. William Lauder, CEO of cosmetics manufacturer Estée Lauder, says, "The challenge for any brand marketer is how to continue to maintain a modernity or contemporaneous look to your brand while not changing it so much that a loyal consumer says, 'It's not my brand anymore.'"

Second, *believability*. Is your positioning plausible on the surface to both internal and external audiences? For a new brand, this usually isn't an issue, but a company that's trying to revive its fortunes must factor into the equation its historical identity.

Years ago, as Burger King began its long night of stalled growth, the company tested upscale dinner items at some of its restaurants. While it may have been somewhat relevant to the evolving target the company was then trying to attract, it just was not believable. How could a fast-food joint do a good job serving steak dinners? Even if it *did*, no one would really believe it. In a similar move, McDonald's tried to sell pizza a few years back and found that this, too, was too much of a stretch for the brand.

Believability is one of the problems caused by pursuing a line-extension strategy. A brand that works great in one category doesn't necessarily work in others. And while you can leverage the power of a brand name into unfamiliar territory up to a point, when you do so, you're slowly diluting its power. Sometimes you can stretch a brand so thin that it rips.

The third positioning test is *credibility*, believability's close cousin. Whereas believability is an analysis from the outside in (can this brand really do that?), credibility is a question to be answered from the inside out (can we deliver what we say?). To be credible, you must be able to execute your staked-out positioning from top to bottom; everything you do (beyond what is traditionally labeled "marketing") must fit with and reinforce it.

I mentioned Ritz-Carlton's commitment to their Somehow strategy of first-rate service. Given their success, it's natural for less-focused hotel chains to try to piggyback onto the same approach, with little understanding of how the principle of distinctiveness works. One chain in which I stayed had recently launched a new slogan that was proudly displayed in its lobby: "Be Hospitable." Yet when I called the front desk to request a late checkout because of a meeting I was attending in *their* conference center, I had to argue with the clerk to get just one additional hour. What do you think I'm going to remember every time I see their promise? A credibility gap, that's what.

Jim McDowell, vice president of marketing at BMW North America, captured the vital importance of credibility when he said, "If you want to be really vivid with precise edges in the marketplace, you have to have the discipline to prune away relentlessly all the things that you're not. Few marketers have this discipline. We can all name the ones who do. And their brands are famous, trusted, and reliable."[20]

Fourth: *differentiation*. Does the prospective positioning set you apart from alternate methods of meeting the need? There's a principle we use as we work with our clients to shape and mold their brand identities: don't be better, be different. That doesn't mean you shouldn't strive to be the best at what you do, but no matter how relevant, believable, credible, and high quality your brand is, if your competitors are claiming the same ground, you'll have to outspend them to make any progress. Parity creates brand confusion, which is usually sorted out by price. But the scarcity brought about by differentiation creates perceived value.

Keep in mind, however, that differentiation, like relevance, can be a moving target. The more success you have, the more your competitors will try to claim the ground you've staked out, which may be why you stalled in the first place. If your evolving positioning will still require you to claim that your brand is better than (as opposed to different from) its competitors, it has a differentiation deficit.

Fifth, *defensibility*. Even if a prospective positioning passes all of the above tests, it won't do any good if a competitor can swoop in and take it from you. That's why it's important to focus on a narrow position and defend it with everything you've got. That will enable you to build barriers to entry. Joe Mansueto, founder of Morningstar, the respected investment research company, describes high barriers to entry as "a 'moat' that shields [companies] from competition and allows them to earn high rates of return." Mansueto is constantly on the lookout for innovations that "deepen" the moat.[21]

If you can develop (or refine) a positioning that passes all five of the above tests, you'll really be onto something. It will enable you to pursue your "I" with nerve and verve. Remember the three symptoms of a loss of nerve from Chapter 6? Building a distinctive positioning, to serve a specific target, in pursuit of a clear Top Box is the best possible way to overcome them. Here's how:

Fear of risk. Both fear and risk are based on the unknown, and the more you know, the more they can be overcome. Setting a clear goal, intimately understanding your target, and creating powerful meaning behind your brand will replace fear with confidence. When Hyundai introduced its ten-year warranty, it looked risky to outsiders (including me), but insiders knew that the quality of its cars had sufficiently improved to make the claim credible. And it turned around the company's fortunes in the United States. (I even bought one for my daughter.)

Resistance to change. The marketing equation is a step-by-step, logical framework that will enable you to differentiate good change from bad change. If the analysis reinforces your existing target and positioning, it may be that your problems are related to temporary tectonics. If so, like Marion McGovern at M^2, you can do what you need to ride it out. But if competition has overtaken your positioning, or changing dynamics have forever altered your customer profile, you'll determine (as Kodak did when it moved to digital imaging) that it's time to take action.

Reluctance to spend. A market-driven positioning arrived at through the application of proven marketing principles will create internal excitement and will reignite a desire among your team to go for it. As Morningstar's Mansueto says, "Once you spot opportunity and you're convinced your reasoning is correct, you move boldly."[22]

With your Top Box in place, your target in sight, and your positioning clarified, that's all you have left to do.

13

Let It Fly

Your marketing equation is almost complete. You have a clearly defined Top Box, which everyone on your team understands and supports. You have done your homework and developed a target insight profile that is deep and revealing. And you have discovered (or confirmed) a niche in the marketplace to which you are going to commit your brand wholeheartedly. Now all you have to do is draw back the bow and let your arrow fly.

It's as simple, and as difficult, as that.

A few years ago, I was driving down the interstate in my hometown and had an eye-opening realization. I don't remember the date, but I know it was winter because that's the only time of the year when a thin layer of haze occasionally hugs the Albuquerque cityscape instead of dissipating into the atmosphere. During the morning rush hour that day, the haze turned brown from the exhaust fumes and dust kicked up by the traffic.

Albuquerque straddles the beautiful Rio Grande valley, with mile-high mountains towering just to the east. When you're in the center of town, near the river, you don't even notice the haze, much as commuters in Los Angeles are oblivious to the smog that surrounds them. But driving along the edge of town, as I was that day, gave me a bird's-eye perspective on the dirty air into which I would soon be descending.

As the freeway wove its way down into the valley, I noticed up in the distance a truck of some kind spewing black smoke out of its exhaust pipe. It wasn't stalled at the side of the road, a victim of some engine malfunction; it was just plodding along as if nothing was wrong. The sight of the truck and its filthy exhaust made me angry. "This is the problem," I thought. "Most cars these days run relatively clean, but polluters like this are what spoil our air."

As I drew nearer, I noticed it was some sort of delivery truck, and realizing that it was probably on the streets all day, every day, only frustrated me more. Soon I had caught up with the truck and, not wanting to directly inhale its foul exhaust, I pulled alongside to pass. I was stunned by the big blue logo proudly displayed on the side panel: Crystal Springs Bottled Water.

Crystal Springs is a leading local provider of clean, pure bottled water. The company is a member of the International Bottled Water Association (IBWA) and follows the IBWA Model Code as the basis for its quality control program. It maintains "Bottled Water Plant Certification" from the National Sanitation Foundation and has strict production standards, patterned after U.S. Food and Drug Administration guidelines. The company voluntarily subjects itself to unannounced inspections by the local Environmental Health Department and unannounced third parties.[1] Crystal Springs makes a good, clean bottle of water and uses creative, award-winning advertising to make sure people know it.

I couldn't help but shake my head as I zoomed past the offending delivery truck. All the time, money, and energy the company had been spending building an image in my mind based on purity was going up in smoke (exhaust, technically). And it wasn't just me; hundreds, if not thousands, of other drivers had been exposed to the same offense. "What was the company thinking?" I wondered aloud to myself. "Do they just not notice? Or worse, do they not care?"

It's possible that my maddening experience with the Crystal Springs truck was a one-time event and that as soon as the driver realized what was happening, he had the vehicle serviced and the problem corrected. I certainly hope so. But either way, the lesson was driven home to me that day: whatever good branding births, poor execution can kill.

Execution Is Everything

On that cold winter morning, it didn't matter how good Crystal Springs water tasted. It didn't matter how clever the company's advertising was. It didn't matter how nice a guy the man driving the truck was, what his on-time performance was, or how pleasantly he chatted with office managers when he made his deliveries. What mattered that day was how "off-brand" my experience with the truck was. Chances are, the company never even knew it.

One of my favorite quotations is from legendary newsman Edward R. Murrow. He said, "Our major obligation is not to mistake slogans for solutions."[2] When growth stalls, it's easy to focus on correcting or changing the most visible things, like ads and taglines. But rarely are marketing issues the sole problem; poor marketing didn't get you into this mess, and great marketing alone won't get you out. Nor will creating a smart, strategic, innovative plan. "Without execution," says Mark Hurd, CEO of Hewlett-Packard, "vision is just another word for hallucination."[3]

Hurd knows something of what he speaks. Taking over HP at a time of confusion and upheaval, when the company had acquired but not yet integrated Compaq, Hurd improved market share (surpassing Dell as the number one PC manufacturer in the world) and raised profitability. In fact, he led HP to revenue-per-worker that was twice that of IBM.[4] The incredible performance of Hurd and his team led one analyst to call HP "an execution machine."[5]

As is Neiman Marcus. The company knows that the key to its success is staying laser-focused on its well-heeled customers and doing whatever it takes to please them. As a result, it invests in the customer experience. This includes decorating the stores with beautiful artwork—lots of it—ranging from fine artists discovered in the regions around their stores to great masters like Picasso. Store designers consider every detail, from the comfort of their stools to ensuring that chair armrests are long enough so that customer purses can be hung from them. And they prefer to hire full-time employees, keeping part-timers to a minimum.

Employees are indoctrinated into the Neiman Marcus way through 200 hours of initial training, followed by 160 more hours annually. The training helps them master the art of forming relationships with their clients, earning permission to call them about upcoming events or new merchandise arrivals. "When you serve customers who can buy anything they want," says Ignaz Gorischek, "giving them an experience they can't buy anywhere else is essential." Gorischek is vice president of visual planning and presentation at Neiman Marcus, a title that itself reveals how intensely the company focuses on execution.[6]

David Nadler is vice chairman of consulting firm Marsh & McLennan and a former faculty member at Columbia University's graduate school of business. He has studied organizational change extensively and is the author of *Champions of Change: How CEOs and Their Companies Are Mastering the Skills of Radical Change* (1997, Jossey-Bass). Nadler explains the principle behind this last piece of the puzzle succinctly: "Most failures have nothing to do with strategy. Most hinge on execution."[7]

Companies that emerge from periods of stalled growth understand that Marshall McLuhan's famous quip, "The medium is the message," now extends to every facet of the enterprise, not just its public persona. Harvard's Michael Porter makes the point as well: "The whole matters more than any individual part. Competitive advantage grows out of the entire system of activities."[8]

Porter demonstrates his thinking through the example of probability compounding. If there's a 90 percent chance that a competitor can match you in any one activity, then the chance they can match you in two is 81 percent, while the probability of matching you in three is only 66 percent. The point is that the more consistently you execute within your chosen niche, the more difficult you will be to overtake. "It is harder for a rival to match an array of interlocked activities," he says, "than it is merely to imitate a particular sales-force approach, match a process technology, or replicate a set of product features. Positions built on systems of activities are far more sustainable than those built on individual activities."[9]

Your team's task at this stage of the process is to create or refine the "array of interlocked activities" that makes your company distinctive from the competition and compellingly attractive to your target. You are refining the "X" in the "I choose X" equation.

That's what Frank Blake, CEO of Home Depot, knows he must do to revive the struggling retailer as he closes underperforming stores, hires more experienced salespeople, increases the number of workers on the floor, and improves merchandise management.[10] Still, commenting on a program that solicits grades about headquarters from Home Depot store managers, Blake said, "It's a great thing, but unfortunately our scores are not very good. If a store got the same score, we would consider it underperforming, and we would be flipping out."[11] Blake sees that his company has a way to go in once again executing well on the second half of its "You can do it. We can help" slogan. "There are times," he says, "when an associate sees a customer looking at a particular merchandise display and he or she may not really know much about that particular product. The inclination is to walk by. That's our problem here in headquarters in terms of not giving them adequate training. We're trying to fix that."[12]

Blake has his work cut out for him, as do you and I and every other manager in a company that is trying to generate consistent, long-term growth. Execution isn't something we do once. It's not an accomplishment we can look back on with satisfaction. We can't, in fact, look back on execution at all. It's something we have to do all day, every day, without end. That's why it's so difficult to do well.

Three-Dimensional Consistency

When it comes to the "X" part of the marketing equation, consistency is vital in three areas. First, you must execute your positioning consistently across the entire organization. Second, you must execute your strategy consistently over time. And third, you must invest consistently in keeping your brand distinctive.

To begin with, your team must remember the "I" axiom—it doesn't matter what we think, all that matters is what they think—and view their respective functions through the eyes of your target prospects, aligning the company's value equation with their needs and wants. Your product, packaging, service, décor, shipping, return policy, financing terms, staffing, inventory management, quality control, invoicing, telephone support, advertising, on-hold message, parking lots, delivery trucks, uniforms, and anything else that impacts the brand (and remember, that's everything) must be designed and delivered in keeping with what will delight your customers and prospects.

It's easy to hold up as examples brands on the luxury end of the spectrum: Neiman Marcus, Tiffany, Lexus. They have the margins and the motivation to pay acute attention to the wants and whims of those they serve. But there are powerful examples at the low end of the market as well. While it was partly a function of Sam Walton's legendary thrift, the fact that Walmart's store designs are simple and nondescript reinforces the customers' belief that they're getting the cheapest price available.

Southwest Airlines also understands how to execute consistently. Everything the company does supports the idea of low prices and friendly service. Southwest was the first airline to figure out that while its flight attendants have to deliver the Federal Aviation Administration's required safety instructions over the intercom, they didn't have to stick rigidly to the script, and some of the airline's amateur Lettermans are actually quite funny. And don't think the airline serves peanuts because it can't afford pretzels or crackers; the snack is just one more opportunity to reinforce the point that Southwest charges "peanuts" for its fares. The company's consistent execution extends even to its fuel-hedging strategy, which, as of this writing, has made it the only consistently profitable airline in the face of unprecedented fuel price increases. In 2008, when United, American, Delta, and other competitors announced that they were going to nickel-and-dime passengers by charging them for "excess" baggage, Southwest quickly took out full-page ads in national newspapers saying "Fees Don't Fly with Us."[13] That's the advantage of knowing who you are and what you stand for.

As you commit to a new or refined direction in the quest for renewed growth, every element of your company's operation should be on the table for scrutiny. Manufacturing, R&D, sales, customer service—each department should be pulled apart and put back together again in a way that maximizes its contribution to your distinctive positioning. Turf battles and old arguments over strategies, tactics, and budgets may not have entirely dissipated, but with a clear objective, a well-defined target, and a powerful positioning in mind, you will have established a forum for reasonable debate and a set of meaningful criteria for making the tough decisions wisely.

O-E-O-E-O . . .

No, it's not a refrain from *The Wizard of Oz*, "Old McDonald Had a Farm," or Morris Day and The Time. O-E-O-E-O is a chain of events that has been affecting your company since the day it was launched and that will be significantly impacted as you commit to this new initiative. O represents the Opinion customers and prospects have about your brand. E represents the Experiences that customers have with your brand. And the O-E-O-E-O chain reflects the fact that one influences the other in an endless cycle of either loyalty-enhancing satisfaction or loyalty-destroying disappointment.

If a prospective customer is completely unaware of your brand, you have a clean slate (until the customer starts doing his or her homework and discovers how well or poorly you have performed in the past). Before you can generate a transaction from this prospect, the customer will have to become aware of your existence and form an initial opinion about you.

This can be driven somewhat by advertising, but many other factors may also be important. They may include articles customers read about your company, D&B reports they pull on you, the signs out in front of store locations they pass, a cold call your sales force makes to them, or even someone in front of them at the checkout line wearing a shirt with your logo on it. (You want to be careful with this. I once witnessed a group of businesspeople being incredibly rude to others in an airport. They were all wearing the same company logo on their polo shirts, which didn't escape their victims' notice.)

In some cases, your prospects' initial opinions will lead them to decide to do business with you ("A five-blade razor? Hmm. . . . I think I'll give it a try."). In other cases, they won't have much choice ("Sorry, you can only use company-approved vendors."). But one way or another, they will form some sort of opinion about your brand and its value equation.

Then comes the experience. They taste your food, wear your clothing, subscribe to your service, pop your top, install your machinery, test-drive your car, load up your software, strap on your shoes, or show up in your office for an initial consultation. Without even consciously knowing it, throughout the course of their experience, they will be processing all of the cues you provide into a sort of mental "brand satisfaction index" that incorporates sights, sounds, smells, textures, and tastes as well as wait times, pricing, service, defect ratios, friendliness, and a host of other factors pertinent to their needs. That experience will be added to what they already knew about your brand, and a revised opinion will be formed. If you've done your homework right and do your job well, that opinion will be new and improved and will generate another experience. That experience will generate another (hopefully improved) opinion, and so on, in a never-ending loop of O-E-O-E-O.

For companies that execute well, the O-E-O-E-O cycle will be music to their ears, leading their prospects to say "I choose you" not just once but again and again. For those that don't, the experience part of the chain will soon come to a halt, and all that will be left is a bad opinion, one that ex-customers are likely to share with others. That's when growth stalls again.

To keep the music playing, you have to execute consistently across the enterprise. But you also have to execute consistently over time.

There are a lot of baseball records that impress me. I couldn't hit one fastball or steal a single base, so the achievements of Ken Griffey, Jr., and Rickey Henderson are amazing to me. But the one record I can identify with is that of Cal Ripken, Jr. He showed up for 2,632 consecutive games, an all-time record. That's eighteen years without missing a single start (plus three more after voluntarily breaking his streak) while performing at a Hall of Fame level throughout. The reason I can identify with Ripken is not because I have his talent (I don't), his focus (I wish), or his bank account (would be nice). It's because I appreciate just how hard it is to perform a complex set of tasks, at a very high level, for such a long period of time. Ripken, like HP and Neiman Marcus, is an execution machine.

Andy Grove, former chairman of Intel, once said, "Brand building is a process that is measured in years, not months."[14] It doesn't matter whether you're selling insurance to consumers or industrial equipment to manufacturers; no matter what kind of business you're in, consistency pays off. Jim Speros is chief marketing officer for Ernst & Young, a past chairman of the Association of National Advertisers, and a twenty-year veteran of AT&T, one of the nation's biggest business-to-business advertisers. He says, "Once you pick a position, it's important to stay the course and not move off of it. All too often, marketers will stay with a position for too short a time. To be a success, a business-to-business marketer needs to be more long-term in its position and stay focused on that."[15]

Like compound interest, the returns on consistency can be small at first but will, over time, grow larger and larger. But the power of compound interest is lost on many savers, as is the power of compound consistency among corporate leaders. Our research shows that stalled companies are four times less likely to maintain a consistent marketing message. Too often, they let panic, hubris, or boredom get the better of wisdom.

Show Me the Money

Perhaps the most difficult part of reigniting growth is putting your money where your mouth is. It's all well and good to navel-gaze while working through the elements of the marketing equation, but when it's time to execute, you find out how much you really believe.

If you're like most of the stalled company leaders we've interviewed, you already know that you're not investing enough in growth. You just haven't had the confidence to do so. Maybe you feel unwilling to throw good money after bad. Perhaps you've been cash poor. But remember, there are two key resources in business: money and time. If you don't have the money, use whatever time is available to you and your employees to begin implementing your plan. Things may not change as quickly as you want, but at this point your goal is to generate some early momentum.

If you do have the money, now is the time to put it to use. If you're confident that your retooled operations are ready to go to market, invest in smart marketing that leverages your point of distinction. If not, invest within.

That's a recommendation we've made more than once to clients who come to us for marketing advice. If we see that their products, prices, or places are out of whack, we tell them not to waste their money on the fourth "marketing P," promotion. As they say, the best way to kill a bad product is with a good ad.

It can be difficult to know exactly when and how much to reinvest in the company, but the marketing equation will reveal where best to spend it. And you must not let the fear of external tectonics stand in your way. During difficult economic times, Denmark's Bang & Olufsen has intentionally increased its R&D funding: "We have actually boosted investments in new projects," said Peter Thostrup, CFO. "Innovation, after all, is a way out of recession."[16] Thanks to the company's aggressive R&D philosophy, it may have two to three dozen new concepts in development at any time, only a third of which will turn into real products. But those few innovations may include a couple of blockbusters that will drive company growth for years to come.

Home Depot's Blake agrees. "Don't be afraid to invest in the business during a downturn," he says. "You'll be in a position of strength when the economy recovers."[17]

What About the Fourth P?

As a consultant who works with a wide variety of companies in a diverse array of industries, I benefit from cross-pollination of experiences and ideas. I get to witness many different challenges to growth, to share in the development of an equal number of growth plans, and to witness firsthand what works, what doesn't, and why.

While every company's story is unique, I have seen the marketing equation work time and time again as companies focus their brands on a singular goal, a singular target, and a singular market position. That said, I am a marketing consultant, and I claim no special expertise in the financial or operational issues facing my clients. Regenerating growth is a team effort, and although my firm plays a key role, we play only one role.

Beyond the overarching perspective my firm brings to struggling companies that seek us out, however, we do give them pretty good advice on the fourth "P": promotion. A chapter on execution wouldn't be complete, in my mind, without touching on that.

Much can be said about the issue of marketing communications, but the most succinct advice I could provide is this: your marketing efforts aren't *about* you; they're an *extension* of you.

Here's what I mean. If you could personally reach out and talk with each and every one of your prospective customers, relate to them as individuals, and lovingly introduce them to your product or service, you would. That may be possible for, say, a company like Boeing or Airbus that sells multibillion-dollar airplanes to a short list of several dozen customers. But Wendy's, which needs to generate some three hundred million or more transactions every year, has a more difficult challenge in doing so. Wendy's ads, like those of most companies, are its proxy, effectively extending the company's reach into the homes of people who will never meet a company executive face-to-face.

But the basis of that outreach should be no different than in a personal encounter. Advertising is like any other form of human interaction. It should be couched, first and foremost, in respect for its audience. That pretty much rules out shouting, lying, and the trashing of competitors. And it means that your advertising should be warm, funny, touching, inspirational, or engaging in some other form. In other words, it should reward the audience for paying attention.

The reason is simple. Advertising is as much a part of the O-E-O-E-O chain as any other form of experience with your brand. It's much less powerful in forming opinions than actual purchase experiences, but it can touch people more frequently. You want to build a relationship with customers when they place an order, come into your stores, or take delivery of your merchandise, and your advertising should serve the same purpose.

We have an assessment that serves as a good early-stage filter for the marketing messages we have in development. We call it the "Reception Test."

Have you ever been cornered at a corporate reception or cocktail party by someone really annoying? Perhaps he's scanning the room, looking for someone better to meet while tying up your attention. Or maybe he's boring you with inane facts about his resume, accomplishments, degrees, kids, job, or whatever. When someone is that rude or self-absorbed, your impression of him will not be good, and you'll probably avoid him the next time you see him. A lot of advertising is like that guy.

Other times, however, you'll meet someone at a reception with whom you genuinely connect. You may find yourself engaged in a fascinating conversation, sharing a humorous observation, or discovering that you have something meaningful in common. Sometimes those conversations evolve into business relationships and even friendships. Some advertising works like that.

If you've been in business for any length of time, you've learned reception etiquette. You know you should focus on one person at a time. You understand the importance of making eye contact and listening. You know to avoid talking too much about yourself; instead, you try to discover what they're interested in. Most of all, you make sure not to be arrogant, boorish, or annoying. Following these simple rules increases your chances of starting an interesting new relationship. Beyond that, they're just plain polite.

Believe it or not, the same rules apply to advertising.

Think about how you relate to most ads you see. You expect them to focus on themselves (in the form of product attributes, company characteristics, or even self-aggrandizing cleverness for its own sake). You expect them to be loud. You expect them to tell you what they want you to hear rather than focusing on what's interesting to you. Most ads act like someone with bad manners at a reception. In short, they fail the Reception Test.

That's why most advertising underperforms. Advertisers desperately want to have a relationship with their prospects, but the reverse doesn't usually hold true. And the more an advertiser presses, the less likely it is that their message will be well received. Just like at a reception or cocktail party, advertisers have to win people over, not bowl them over.

There is a great deal of debate about the entertainment value of advertising and whether an ad should strive to entertain or simply focus on selling. In my mind, it's a false argument. All purchase occasions can be considered a form of entertainment for the buyer; even such challenging assignments as finding the right new car or specifying a new computer platform for your company can be rewarding, especially if the outcome is positive. Thus, all sales occasions require an attempt at entertainment from the seller; ask anyone who has ever sold for a living, and they'll tell you how vital their relationship skills are to the process.

Effective marketing communications are 100 percent about likability: helping the buyer to like *what* you offer as well as *who* you are. Loosely translated, that parallels your brand positioning and your brand personality, respectively, and the stalled companies we studied report deficits in both. Contrary to what the "loyalty marketing" experts who peddle points and miles say, all marketing is loyalty marketing.

This is another facet of consistency. Think about how you respond to marketing as a consumer. Do you ever feel compelled to rush out and buy something simply because you saw it advertised? Usually not. It can take a while for an advertising idea to sink in. People have to be exposed to the message over time, and they have to come to a point where their awareness of the product and trust in the brand align with their needs and natural purchase cycle. And that happens on their schedule, not ours. Companies seeking to maintain consistent growth know that marketing is a marathon, not a sprint.

When it comes to executing the communications piece of your puzzle, follow legendary ad man Bill Bernbach's advice: "Find the simple story in the product, and present it in an articulate and intelligent, persuasive way." Do it with excellence, do it throughout the enterprise, and do it consistently. When you do, you'll be well on your way to achieving your Top Box.

14

It Works

There's a chance that at this point you're saying, "This is too simplistic." Perhaps you're shaking your head, eyebrows furrowed, convinced that your company is too big, too complex, too sophisticated, or too unusual; that you have too many business units, too many diverse audiences, or too many pricing tiers to be subject to the simplicity of the marketing equation.

You can complicate things all you want with spreadsheets, regression analyses, market studies, copy testing, multinationalism, or anything else, but it does not change the fact that the marketing equation rules the day. Whether your target is a CEO in the boardroom determining the fate of a multibillion-dollar contract, or a parent in the supermarket deciding between two boxes of cereal, your task is to understand your audience, determine what they're looking for, and align your product or service with their wants and needs. Do that consistently, and you'll achieve your Top Box. Don't and, well, you won't.

On the other hand, perhaps you're smiling in anticipation, believing the marketing equation will make turning things around and returning to healthy growth a piece of cake. But the fact that it's simple doesn't mean it's easy. And while in principle the marketing equation is straightforward, in application it's a bit more difficult. The most basic mistake you could make is to shortcut the process, skip a step, or try to address the variables out of order. Do that, and no matter how sleek your rocket ship appears, it will never get off the launching pad.

Either way, the best way I can sum it all up is with an example of a company that is rewriting the rules of its industry using the principles of the marketing equation: Charles Luck Stone Center. The company isn't a client of ours, and until I met the president, he had never heard of the principles I espouse, at least in the form that I espouse them. But the leadership at Charles Luck has mastered the marketing equation nonetheless, and their results speak for themselves. The company has applied these principles so well and so consistently that the odds of their avoiding the specter of stalled growth are very good indeed.

Charles Luck Stone Center is one of four companies in the Luck Stone family of businesses owned by a privately held, Richmond, Virginia–based organization that provides natural stone in raw and finished form to regional, national, and international clients in the architectural, construction, and consumer sectors. With a variety of quarries and retail locations in North Carolina and Maryland as well as Virginia, Luck Stone generates hundreds of millions of dollars in revenue each year.

Mark Fernandes is president of Charles Luck Stone Center. Eighteen years ago, he "barely graduated" from North Carolina State University. ("I was a nontraditional student," he says. "I never went to class.") Then a chance meeting at a gym led Fernandes to become a stonemason at Luck Stone. He worked his way through operations, tried his hand at sales, moved up through the ranks to become vice president, and today is the visionary behind an incredible transformation.

But he's not alone. Charlie Luck, the company's namesake and third-generation chairman, has big visions himself. Fernandes says Luck "has no interest in having a status quo company; he really is interested in reinventing business that'll have a societal impact, and he's very sincere about that. We're fortunate that we have an owner who is passionate about doing things differently." That's evident by the process Luck and Fernandes have implemented to keep innovation at the heart of the organization.

It began in the mid-1990s with "Vision 2000," a blueprint for expanding the company geographically. Then came "Vision 2005," which was all about the integration of inventory management, back-office, and retail technology throughout the organization. That wasn't a slam dunk, given the low-tech industry in which the company competes. But they got it done, and with two successes under their belt, they embarked in 2003 on "Vision 2010."

In addition to Luck and Fernandes, the Vision 2010 team included a vice president of strategic development, John Pullen, who Fernandes describes as "one of those see-around-the-corner guys who really challenges conventional thinking." Fernandes said the company had formerly outsourced the strategic planning part of the equation to external consultants, but once the process became part of the fabric of the company, they brought it inside. Understanding the importance of consensus, the team included the heads of operations, sales, marketing, human resources, information technology, and a handful of other key players. The goal, according to Fernandes, was to make the team as cross-functional as possible. That ensured that whatever they discovered (and whatever implications came with it) would be understood and embraced throughout the organization.

Because the team was engaged in a rolling planning process, they didn't need to spend much time on the Top Box. Their overarching definition of success was clear from day one: to be a values-based company with world-class strategic agility delivering sustained top-line and margin growth. As such, they were quickly able to embark on the discovery phase.

And discovery was what the process was all about. They knew that they couldn't take Luck Stone's historical business model for granted; everything had to be on the table, and team members were encouraged to challenge not only industry conventions but their own assumptions as well. Fernandes says their objectives were to "use our heads *and* guts, think both linearly *and* conceptually, dig for opportunities under the radar, look for seemingly unrelated ideas," and importantly, "look for unfulfilled needs, wants, and desires" among their customers and prospects.

It began inside. "The very first thing we always do," says Fernandes, "is start with our associates, talking with them about what's working and what's not, what's making them crazy and what their dreams are. Then we go out and start our focus on the marketplace." That includes a comprehensive scan of market tectonics, both visible and invisible.

Says Fernandes about that time, "If you were paying attention, you could certainly see the writing on the wall with the competition." His team recognized not only increasing competitive activity from overseas imports, but also changing dynamics brought about by the introduction of manufactured alternative materials (think Corian and Silestone). They also knew that they wouldn't always be able to count on what at that time was a booming home-building industry.

Their discovery phase was an exercise in future-casting. They read trend-spotting authors like Malcolm Gladwell (*The Tipping Point* and *Blink*), James Gilmore (*The Experience Economy*), and Daniel Pink (*A Whole New Mind*); noted the proliferation of design and fashion programs on television (*Project Runway*, *America's Next Top Model*); and saw that art topped wine in "cool factor" surveys.[1] They studied great brands, from Coca-Cola to Ralph Lauren. And they carefully examined both the present state and future prospects of their key target audiences, including consumers and the design and architectural communities. As Fernandes put it, their goal was to "lift the covers and find the truth of what really matters."

Lifting those covers provided a breakthrough insight to the Luck Stone planning team: They discovered an "I"—a valuable segment of the buying public—that appreciated and could afford the company's stone products but were highly dissatisfied with the traditional buying process. That spelled opportunity.

Fernandes says their research showed that the luxury end of the home-building market had grown 600 percent in five years. "Everybody, no matter what their price point is, wants to feel good about themselves," he says. "But the higher up the food chain we went toward luxury, we saw a big hole." Fernandes and his team uncovered a segment of customers that wanted to feel stylish and smart when building or renovating their homes, to express themselves individually, to be creative and unique, and to feel that way not just after the product was installed but through the entire purchase experience. Pondering this target, the team saw opportunity in a Somehow strategy.

Over the course of nearly two years, the Luck Stone team's research led them to conclude that their biggest opportunity lay in reorienting the company toward this luxury market, and to do so in a big way. Their vision became "to create a destination for people who appreciate things of enduring value and the experience of acquiring them." Or in more colloquial terms, to evolve "from Fred Flintstone to fashion-forward." But instead of jumping straight to execution, as many companies would, they first studied how best to fulfill the "choose" variable of the marketing equation. If luxury customers were the people they wanted, they were going to learn how to treat them from the best.

They studied Ritz-Carlton and its famous service model. They explored the mix of art and commerce at leading museums around the world. They scrutinized retail models, as Fernandes says, "from Manhattan to Milan." They even hired a consultant from Saks Fifth Avenue to understand "the way that you answer the phones, the way you greet a client, and the importance of privacy." And they outlined a fivefold execution plan to ensure that their "X" would be consistent throughout the O-E-O-E-O cycle, encompassing people, places, products, processes, and promotion. All five, Fernandes and his team knew, had to be in alignment.

Luck Stone had historically obtained stone from all over the world in addition to its own quarries. They had contacts in every corner of the globe who could help them identify slabs not only for their unique form and function but for the stories behind them.

Unlike a lot of building materials, stone comes from a *place*—a place with its own history and heritage. Just considering granite countertops alone, Luck Stone sells such varied exotic materials as Verde Marinace from Brazil, Silver Quartzite from Italy, Costa Esmeralda from Spain, Absolute Black from Africa, and Baltic Brown from Finland. Even the names suggest artistry, romance, and glamour—qualities most people wouldn't associate with the stone-cutting business but that Luck Stone's high-end customers craved.

That inspired the Luck Stone team to create a brand of their own, an exclusive new line of stone designs available only through their retail locations. Viewing stone as a fashion statement, they began rolling out new designs with each new season, much the way designers like Calvin Klein and Tommy Hilfiger continuously move fashion trends forward. That gave them a product strategy that would keep them not only distinctive but ever evolving.

Their thoughts then turned to the physical locations in which their customers would be romanced. Fernandes and his team re-thought every element of the sales process and broke many of the conventions of the retail stone industry. They decided to call their stores studios rather than sales floors or showrooms, and designed a prototype reminiscent of a warm, well-kept modern farmhouse or hunting lodge. Each studio featured art on the walls instead of pictures of stone kitchens or fireplaces, and forsook the expected vignettes and outdoor living displays. It incorporated hardwood floors, high ceilings, a judicious and tasteful use of stone, and lots of natural light.

The walls were designed to house sliding floor-to-ceiling panels of sixteen-inch-by-sixteen-inch samples of Luck Stone's exclusive product line, providing hundreds of color and texture options at customers' fingertips. The studios stocked an inventory of custom-designed, coaster-sized stone samples that matched the products on the wall so customers could feel and touch the stone, compare and contrast different pieces on the design tables, and take them home to see how they interacted with the colors, textures, and lighting patterns there.

Each oblong design table was crafted to foster collaboration, with eight comfortable stools and a cabinet at one end that housed a computer and DVD player that designers could use to show videos about the history and heritage of the pieces (and where customers could go online or even check their own e-mail, if they so desired). The design goal of the physical environment was all about making guests feel as comfortable, and as welcome to linger, as they would in the well-appointed home of a friend.

The Luck Stone team knew, however, that their task was as much about the experience as it was the physical place. "Everything we do," says Fernandes, "had to be targeted at that niche, from the language we used to the behaviors we exhibited." The team crafted a plan to create "brand ambassadors" whose sole objective was to make customers feel welcome, wanted, and unhurried. Working with the consultant from Saks, Luck Stone devoted 120 of the 200 days leading up to the first studio's opening to training, with each staff member immersed in the new way of doing things for 6 to 8 full days. Says Fernandes, "If part of your brand is to have Crabtree & Evelyn in the bathroom, it has to be there 100 percent of the time, not 99 percent."

Then came promotion. It actually started with the name. At the time, the retail division was still called Luck Stone, the same name as the company's other operations. It had naturally been tagged with the Luck Stone brand after having emerged out of the much older quarry operations. Back then, having the retail operation tied to the name of the quarry was no big deal.

But Fernandes was concerned that Luck Stone's association with the quarry could potentially confuse its luxury customers as the brand went increasingly upscale. He wanted a name that was reflective of the company's heritage but that could become a respected fashion brand in its own right. After a comprehensive (and expensive) analysis, they settled on a name not far from the company's origins: Charles Luck Stone Center. This would anchor the brand in the respected family name while also communicating exactly what the new brand was about. (Fernandes's goal is to one day be known as simply "Charles Luck," much as the brand names Ralph Lauren and Vera Wang need no further explanation.)

They eschewed most traditional advertising in newspapers and magazines, understanding that the editorial environment in which their ads would appear would reflect on their message. Instead, they took another page from the fashion industry and pursued an event-driven strategy through which they could showcase their new design studio.

It began on a Friday evening with a charity gala and art auction. The highlight of the evening was the auctioning off of a stone mosaic created by Francesca "Tule" Cestarollo, a world-renowned artist from Verona, creating a natural tie-in to the products being showcased. Six hundred well-heeled patrons attended. Fernandes was determined to keep things very low key. "It's not about selling a product," he says. "It's about hosting a really nice gala. And oh, by the way, it just happens to be at the studio where the product and space are all around them."

On another evening, luxury retailer Fink's Jewelers hosted a private event at Charles Luck Stone Center for eighty couples that represented the cream of their customer crop. The event was a showcase of the newest John Hardy jewelry designs, and the Charles Luck design tables offered a perfect way to display the merchandise. Like the charity gala, this event was not about selling stone but about politely introducing customers to the beautiful showroom. Clearly cognizant of the Reception Test, Fernandes and his team politely socialized, letting their stunning environment do the talking for them.

A few weekends later, Fernandes and his team launched "Stone Fashion Week," kicking it off with an event for some three hundred designers and architects. This time it was all about celebrating stone. Fernandes showcased forty designs from his new stone brand while guests enjoyed fabulous catering and admired models mingling with the crowd wearing Saks' spring fashion line. The evening ended with a stunning seven-minute video that celebrated the history and passion surrounding natural stone. It wasn't a commercial for Charles Luck Stone Center; it was, Fernandes says, "an MTV-quality, Pink Floyd–esque video set in cathedrals, the pyramids, and Easter Island." Following the video, Fernandes took the stage and spent a mere seventeen seconds making his pitch: "We are privileged," he began, "to represent what we believe is one of the most important and prolific products in the world, natural stone. It is our intention, from this point forward, to bring the world of stone to you, the design community, for the purpose of inventive design in sustainable construction. Thank you for spending your evening with us."

That was it. The rest of the week was filled with professional design workshops where those who had been wowed on the weekend came to learn more about the Charles Luck product line. For Fernandes it also involved taking a lot of calls from the press, who had been both impressed and somewhat mystified by the company's new business model. Charles Luck Stone Center found itself being compared with Gucci and Prada in stories that carried headlines like, "Making Stone Sexy," "Celebration of Stone," and "Polished to a Shine." That suited Fernandes just fine and equipped his outside sales force with plenty to talk about for the rest of the year as they called on custom builders, landscapers, masons, and the design community.

Just months into the new strategy, it could already be pronounced an unqualified success. Charles Luck Stone Center attracted more than five thousand designers and luxury homeowners during the launch phase, resulting in significant sales and margin growth. Calling it "demand creation," Fernandes and his team have seen firsthand what the marketing equation can do. "We're trying to inspire more choices around natural stone," he says, "and provide all the necessary tools in house designers and a great space in which to do it."

Charles Luck Stone Center did it right. They built consensus and clarity into the system with their continuous planning model. They developed a clear vision of the "I" they would serve, giving them the nerve to align every aspect of their operations around their target. And they focused relentlessly on execution, letting no element of the enterprise go unexamined.

Was it easy? By no means. But it was simple, in the most elegant sense of that word. Fernandes now shares his story with groups anywhere and everywhere who will listen, trying to inspire them with the message that, whatever their business model, they can follow the same principles to success. But he knows most won't. "They just don't see the opportunity," he says. "I really wish they would; we are living proof of the difference you can make."

What about you? Your company may be in bad shape, but there could be a silver lining to your current difficulties if they give you and those around you the willingness and motivation to create significant and permanent change.

Fred Mitchell, British director of the China Inland Mission in the mid-twentieth century, wrote a letter to a young minister that contained sage advice: "It does not matter what happens to us," Mitchell wrote, "but our reaction to what happens to us is of vital importance."[2] Or as Intel's Andy Grove put it: "Nothing sharpens the awareness of a situation like the sight of a gallows."[3]

What will your reaction to stalled growth be? The complexities of the business world make it impossible to plan for every contingency. But by better understanding the tectonic events buffeting your organization and their debilitating internal effects, you can turn things around. Align your team and find your target. Focus your brand and execute consistently. Mean something to the marketplace, and the marketplace will reward you.

When it does, I'd love to hear about it.

Notes

Introduction

1. Kesmodel, D. "For Fortune Brands CEO, Loss Is Win." *Wall Street Journal*, Apr. 11, 2008, B7.

Chapter 1

1. McKee Wallwork Henderson Advertising. "The Four Horses." Self-published, n.d.

Chapter 2

1. Collins, J., and Porras, J. *Built to Last.* New York: HarperCollins, 1994, p. 3.
2. "McDonald's Punished After U.S. Sales Come in Flat in Dec." *USA Today* (Jan. 28, 2008). Retrieved June 17, 2008, from http://www.usatoday.com/money/companies/earnings/2008–01–28-mcdonalds_N.htm.
3. Hamel, G., and Välikangas, L. "The Quest for Resilience." *Harvard Business Review*, Sept. 1, 2003, 2.
4. "Dell Raises New Fears About PC Market." *Wall Street Journal*, May 28, 2001, A3.
5. Lawton, C. "A Look at Dell's Bottom Line Amid Challenging Times." *Wall Street Journal*, Feb. 24, 2007, A2.
6. Helman, C. "The Second Coming." *Forbes.com* (Dec. 10, 2007). Retrieved June 17, 2008, from http://www.forbes.com/forbes/2007/1210/078.html.
7. Lloyd, M. E. "Home Depot Gives Gloomy Outlook." *Wall Street Journal*, Feb. 26, 2008, B5.
8. Cheng, A. "Home Depot Net Falls 24% on Lower Sales." *Wall Street Journal*, Aug. 20, 2008, B5.
9. Frazier, M. "Home Depot CMO: We Need to 'Start All Over'; Q&A: Roger Adams Wants Retailer to Refocus Efforts on Service, Other Basics." (CMO Strategy) (Interview). *Advertising Age*, Oct. 15, 2007, null.
10. Background on Home Depot: various interviews.

11. Frazier, M. "Home Depot Seeks CMO—But, Please, No Rock Stars." (News) (CMOs). *Advertising Age,* Oct. 22, 2007, null.
12. "Growth Companies—The World's Top 200." (n.d.). Retrieved June 26, 2008, from www.deloitte.com/top200/leverage/htm.
13. See note 3.
14. Rosenzweig, P. "The Halo Effect, and Other Managerial Delusions." *McKinsey Quarterly* (Feb. 1, 2008). Retrieved June 18, 2008, from http://www.mckinseyquarterly.com/The_halo_effect_and_other_managerial_delusions_1928.

Chapter 3

1. "Earthquake Summary." (n.d.). Retrieved June 27, 2008, from http://earthquake.usgs.gov/eqcenter/eqinthenews/2008/us2008ryan/#summary.
2. Clark, D. "Sun Microsystems Cuts Jobs as Sales Fall." *Wall Street Journal,* Oct. 8, 2001, A19.
3. Lawton, C. "Sun Micro Record $34 Million Loss." *Wall Street Journal,* May 2, 2008, B3. Clark, D. "Sun Micro Slashes Jobs." *Wall Street Journal,* November 15-16, 2008, B5.
4. "Inside the Best and Worst Performers." *Wall Street Journal,* Mar. 10, 2003, R3.
5. Berman, D. K. "The Dawn of Disconnect." *Wall Street Journal,* Oct. 5, 2004, D8.
6. "Shareholder Scoreboard 2003." *Wall Street Journal* (Mar. 9, 2003). Retrieved June 26, 2003, from http://online.wsj.com/public/resources/documents/scoreboard2003.html.
7. Ogg, J. "Chico's FAS, Same Store Sales Still in Tank." *24/7 Wall Street* (Apr. 10, 2008). Retrieved June 27, 2008, from http://www.247wallst.com/2008/04/chicos-fas-same.html.
8. Merrick, A., and Kingsbury, K. "Retailers See Some Relief; View Still Dim." *Wall Street Journal,* Mar. 7, 2008, A3.
9. Kardos, D. "D. R. Horton Pares Loss." *Wall Street Journal,* Aug. 6, 2008, C12.
10. Corkery, M., and Kardos, D. "KB Home Posts Disappointing Results." *Wall Street Journal,* Apr. 1, 2008, B6.
11. Frangos, A., and Wei, L. "REIT Lender Thornburg Sees Collateral Seized." *Wall Street Journal,* Mar. 8, 2008, B1.
12. Zweig, J. "What History Tells Us About the Market." *Wall Street Journal,* Oct. 11–12, 2008, W4.
13. Crossen, C. "Many Have Claimed to Be Recession-Proof, Few Have Managed It." *Wall Street Journal,* Mar. 10, 2008, B1.
14. Buckman, R. "Silicon Valley's Backers Grapple with Era of Diminished Returns." *Wall Street Journal,* Aug. 3, 2006, A1.
15. Kardos, D. "Circuit City Hears More Static." *Wall Street Journal,* Apr. 3, 2008, B4.

16. Neff, J. "Recession Can Be a Marketer's Friend." *Advertising Age*, Mar. 24, 2008, 1.
17. Neff, J. "P&G Takes Laundry Brands in New Directions." *Advertising Age* (Aug. 25, 2008). Retrieved Aug. 26, 2008, from http://adage.com/print ?article_id=130553.
18. Abboud, L., and Silver, S. "Why It's the Worst of Times in the Tale of One Deal." *Wall Street Journal*, Oct. 4, 2007, B1–B2.
19. Ibid.
20. Lloyd, M. E., and Hudson, K. "New CEO's Cost Cuts Pay Off for RadioShack." *Wall Street Journal*, Feb. 28, 2007, C10.
21. Merrick, A. "Kmart Says CEO Conaway Resigned, Adds Post to Plot of Chairman Adamson." *Wall Street Journal*, Mar. 12, 2002, A3.
22. Byron, E. "Can a Re-engineered Kleenex Cure a Brand's Sniffles?" *Wall Street Journal*, Jan. 22, 2007, A1.
23. Warren, S. "Dell's Net Slips, but Revenue Rises." *Wall Street Journal*, Feb. 11, 2005, A3.
24. Laberre, P. "Will the Net Bounce Back?" *Fast Company* (July 2001). Retrieved June 24, 2008, from http://www.fastcompany.com/articles/2001/08/isummit.html?page=0%2C1.
25. Lawton, C. "A Look at Dell's Bottom Line Amid Challenging Times." *Wall Street Journal*, Feb. 24, 2007, A2.
26. Lloyd, M. "That Pottery Barn Isn't So Unique Anymore." *Wall Street Journal*, Feb. 21, 2007, B1.
27. Lyons, D. "Smart and Cute." *Forbes*, Mar. 21, 2007, 40.
28. Gallagher, D. "Palm Reports Loss, Sees More Trouble Amid Its Makeover." *Wall Street Journal*, Dec. 19, 2007, B5. Buckman, R., and Worthen, B. "Apple Positions iPhone as BlackBerry Rival." *Wall Street Journal*, Mar. 7, 2008, B4.
29. Johnson, A., and Lublin, J. "Can Pfizer Deliver a New Prescription?" *Wall Street Journal*, Mar. 4, 2008, B1.
30. Adamy, J. "Restaurants Feel the Bite of Stay-at-Home Moms." *Wall Street Journal*, Mar. 14, 2008, B1.
31. "Qwest Announces Plan to Cut Jobs. *New Mexico Business Weekly* (Mar. 18, 2008). Retrieved June 19, 2008, from http://albuquerque.bizjournals.com/albuquerque/stories/2008/03/17/daily15.html.
32. Zuckerman, G. "For Stock-Picture Firm Getty, the Stock Picture Is Grainy." *Wall Street Journal*, Mar. 2, 2007, C3.
33. Armstrong, D. "Kodak Raises Forecast for Digital Sales." *Wall Street Journal*, Sept. 23, 2004, A3.
34. Bulkeley, W. "Kodak's Fourth Quarter Profit Soared." *Wall Street Journal*, Jan. 31, 2008, A3.
35. Ibid.
36. Freeman, A. "First Eagle Look for Companies 'in Flux.'" *Wall Street Journal*, Nov. 28, 2001, C17.
37. Harper, C., and Onaran, Y. "End Game." *Bloomberg Markets*, Nov. 2008, 20.

Chapter 4

1. Lencioni, P. *The Five Dysfunctions of a Team: A Leadership Fable*. San Francisco: Jossey-Bass, 2002.
2. Neuborne, E. "Case Study, Stung by Slow Sales, Zippo Turns to Brand Extensions." *Inc.com* (Sept. 2004). Retrieved June 19, 2008, from http://www.inc.com/magazine/20040901/casestudy.html.
3. Rohwedder, C., Cimilluca, D., and Passarielly, C. "Retail Giant Carrefour Opens to Change." *Wall Street Journal*, Mar. 6, 2008, B6.
4. "Daimler-Chrysler Chief Explains His 'Digital' Decisions." *Wall Street Journal*, Sept. 24, 1999, B4.
5. Stoller, G. "Doing Business Abroad? Simple Faux Pas Can Sink You." *USA Today*, Aug. 24, 2007, 2B.
6. Franey, J. "Daimler/Chrysler Merger Didn't Work, Says CEO." *Auto News* (n.d.). Retrieved May 16, 2008, from www.autonews.com/apps/pbcs.dll/article?AID=/20080516/ANE02/829069350.
7. "Belly Up to the Whopper Bar." (News) (Burger King Corp.). *Advertising Age*, Mar. 31, 2008, 29.
8. Mullman, J. "Man Flaws: Why Miller and Crispin Couldn't Stop Lite from Stumbling." (News) ("Randy Ransom Resigns from Crispin Porter and Bogusky"). *Advertising Age*, Mar. 26, 2007, 1.
9. Packard, D. "A Day at the Old HP." *Wall Street Journal*, Mar. 15, 2002, C9.
10. Malone, M. "HP-Compaq Mess Isn't All Carly's Doing." *Wall Street Journal*, May 21, 2002, B2.
11. Jargon, J., Karnitschnig, M., and Lublin, J. "How Hershey Went Sour." *Wall Street Journal*, Feb. 23, 2008, B1.
12. Swisher, K. "Who Is Guilty of Killing Off Excite@Home?" *Wall Street Journal*, Oct. 9, 2001, A16.
13. Useem, M. "Leaders Needn't Fear a Great Number Two." *Wall Street Journal*, Oct. 8, 2001, A26.
14. Hammonds, K. "How Google Grows . . . and Grows . . . and Grows. *Fast Company* (n.d.). Retrieved June 20, 2008, from http://www.fastcompany.com/magazine/69/google.html.
15. Drucker, P. "The American CEO." *Wall Street Journal*, Dec. 30, 2004, A8.

Chapter 5

1. Rozhon, T. "Executives Say Neiman-Marcus Is Talking with Potential Buyers." *New York Times* (Mar. 17, 2005). Retrieved June 20, 2008, from http://www.nytimes.com/2005/03/17/business/17retail.html?_r=1&scp=1&sq=Executive%20says%20Neiman-Marcus%20Buyers&st=cse&oref=slogin.
2. "Texas Pacific Group and Warburg Pincus Complete Acquisition of The Neiman-Marcus Group, Inc. BNET (Oct. 6, 2005). Retrieved June 20, 2008, from http://findarticles.com/p/articles/mi_m0EIN/is_2005_Oct_6/ai_n15677438.

3. Byron, E. "Sale of Neiman's Is Latest Sign of Luxury Halo." *Wall Street Journal*, May 3, 2005, B1.

4. Jenkins, H. "A Cure for the Pay Hysteria." *Wall Street Journal*, Apr. 9, 2008, A14.

5. Adamy, J. "How Jim Skinner Flipped McDonald's." *Wall Street Journal*, Jan. 5, 2007, B1.

6. Allen, J., and Zook, C. *Profit from the Core: Growth Strategy in an Era of Turbulence*. New York: Harvard Business School Press, 2001.

7. Effie Awards: Winners Showcase, 2005. "Multiple Strength for Multiple Cats." *Effie Worldwide, Inc.* (n.d.). Retrieved June 20, 2008, from http://www.effie.org/winners/showcase/2005/475.

8. Cringely, R. "What's Next: Do One Thing Right." *Inc.*, June 1, 2003, 59–60.

9. Mangalindan, M. "E-Business: Google to Name CEO as Strategy to Raise Profile." *Wall Street Journal*, June 6, 2001, B1.

10. "The Loophole Factory." *Wall Street Journal*, Apr. 15, 2008, A18.

11. Anand, S. "H&R Block May Be Primed to Rise." *Wall Street Journal*, Feb. 12, 2008, C2. Shwiff, K., and Polluck, L. "H&R Block Loss Narrows on Revenue Growth." *Wall Street Journal*, Mar. 7, 2008, B5.

12. Kardos, D. "H&R Block Swings to Profit with Focus on Core Business." *Wall Street Journal*, July 1, 2008, B4.

13. "Letter from the Chief Executive Officer." *Charles Schwab Corporation 2005 Annual Report* (Mar. 14, 2006). Retrieved June 20, 2008, from http://www.aboutschwab.com/ar2005/SchwabAR05.pdf.

14. Moore, S. "Talking to Chuck." *Wall Street Journal*, July 28, 2007, A9.

15. "Letter to the Stockholders." *Charles Schwab Corporation 2004 Annual Report* (Mar. 14, 2005). Retrieved June 20, 2008, from http://www.aboutschwab.com/ar2004/schwab_2004_ar.pdf.

16. Breen, B. "Practice Your Storytelling." *Fast Company*, Mar. 2005, 67.

17. Covert, J. "Walmart's Chief Says Retailer Needs to Widen Customer Appeal." *Wall Street Journal*, June 6, 2005, retrieved Oct. 10, 2008, from http://online.wsj.com/article/SB111801187381451266.html?mod=mm_hs_marketing_strategy.

18. McKee, S. "How Companies Lose Their Way." *BusinessWeek.com*, July 15, 2005, retrieved Oct. 10, 2008, from http://www.businessweek.com/smallbiz/content/jul2005/sb20050715_369626.htm.

19. Zimmerman, A. "Walmart Sets Out to Prove It's in Vogue." *Wall Street Journal*, Aug. 25, 2005, B1.

20. Hudson, K. "Walmart Aims to Dig Out of Soft Sales Performance." *Wall Street Journal*, Feb. 5, 2007, A2.

21. Vranica, S., and McWilliams, G. "Walmart Chooses Two New Ad Agencies." *Wall Street Journal*, Jan. 13, 2007, A2.

22. Serafin, R. "From Beetle to Bedraggled: Behind VW's Stunning U.S. Decline." *Advertising Age*, Sept. 13, 1993, 16.

23. Naughton, K. "From the New Beetle to—A VW Pickup?" *BusinessWeek*, Aug. 9, 1999, 37.

24. Taylor, E. "VW to Cut Costs to Produce Golf." *Wall Street Journal*, June 9, 2008, B2. Halliday, J. "Volkswagen Drives Off a Cliff—Again; Automaker Forced to Refocus on Bread-and-Butter Models That Suffered During Dubious Move Upscale." *Advertising Age*, Aug. 8, 2005, 1.

25. Halliday, J. "Sales Drivers Wanted." *Advertising Age*, Jan. 15, 2007, 1. Rauwald, C., and Power, S. "VW's Profit Increases; CEO Wagers on Quality." *Wall Street Journal*, Mar. 10, 2007, B5.

26. Power, S. "VW Aims to Triple U.S. Vehicle Sales." *Wall Street Journal*, Sept. 12, 2007, A8.

27. "Why One of the World's Most Respected Automakers Decided to Shift Gears." *Wall Street Journal*, Sept. 17, 1999, C24.

28. Miller, S., and Lundegaard, K. "An Engineering Icon Slips." *Wall Street Journal*, Feb. 4, 2002, B1.

29. Boudette, N., and Ball, J. "Europe's Luxury Cars Show Some Vulnerability." *Wall Street Journal*, Nov. 12, 2002, D3.

30. Halliday, J. "Slow Lane: Mercedes Gets Lapped in the Luxury Race; Quality Issues, Low-End Entries Hurt Image of Former Category Leader" (News). *Advertising Age*, Aug. 15, 2005, 6.

31. Power, S. "Daimler-Chrysler Net Falls 63% Due Mainly to Mercedes Woes." *Wall Street Journal*, Feb. 11, 2005, A2.

32. Crain, R. "Note to Automobile Dealers: Worry About Blurred Adds." *Advertising Age* (Mar. 25, 2002). Retrieved June 24, 2008, from http://adage.com/abstract.php?article_id=52520.

33. Voight, J. "All Roads Lead to Tennessee." *Adweek*, June 6, 1994, 2.

34. Halliday, J. "Losing Its Brand Soul: How Saturn Blew Its Advantage; Seeking to Regain Earlier Position, Automaker Taps Deutsch for $190M Biz." (News) (Deutsch Advertising). *Advertising Age*, Feb. 5, 2007, 4.

35. Boudette, N. "Nardelli Tries to Shift Chrysler's Culture." *Wall Street Journal*, June 18, 2008, B1.

36. Muller, J. "Chrysler's Last Stand." *Forbes*, Nov. 26, 2007, 169.

37. Boudette, N. E., and Kosdrosky, T. "Chrysler's Unconventional Plan: Sell Fewer Models, Increase Profit." *Wall Street Journal*, Feb. 11, 2008, A3.

38. Adamy, J. "At Starbucks, Low-Key Vet Plots Course." *Wall Street Journal*, Mar. 18, 2008, B1.

39. "Starbucks Chairman Laments 'Commoditization.'" *Wall Street Journal*, Feb. 24, 2007, A4.

40. Scott, M. C. "The Peter Lynch Approach." *AAII [American Association of Individual Investors] Journal* (Jan. 2007). Retrieved June 22, 2008, from http://www.csulb.edu/~pammerma/fin382/screener/lynch.htm.

41. White, B., and Vara, V. "Cisco Changes Tack in Takeover Game." *Wall Street Journal*, Apr. 17, 2008, A1.

42. White, B. "VeriSign to Slim Down, Sharpen Its Focus." *Wall Street Journal*, Nov. 12, 2007, A12.

43. Ball, D. "After Buying Binge, Nestlé Goes on a Diet." *Wall Street Journal*, July 23, 2007, A1.

44. Ball, D. "Unilever Must Prove It Is More Than Just the Sum of Its Brands." *Wall Street Journal*, July 29, 2007, A2.

45. Adamy, J. "Feeling Heat, Heinz Chief Defends Turnaround." *Wall Street Journal*, Apr. 24, 2006, A2.

46. Patrick, A. O., and McKay, B. "A Bittersweet Victory?" *Wall Street Journal*, Apr. 11, 2008, C1.

Chapter 6

1. Goleman, D. "Leadership That Gets Results." *Harvard Business Review*, Mar.–Apr. 2000, 78.

2. Ibid.

3. Merrick, A. "Gap's Image Is Wearing Out." *Wall Street Journal*, Dec. 6, 2001, B1.

4. Ibid.

5. Ibid.

6. Lee, L. "Too Many Surveys, Too Little Passion?" *BusinessWeek*, Aug. 1, 2005, 38.

7. Merrick, A., and Berman, D. "What's Next for Gap?" *Wall Street Journal*, Jan. 9, 2007, C5.

8. Merrick, A. "Gap Aims to Unleash Creativity for Revival." *Wall Street Journal*, Mar. 6, 2007, B2.

9. Jenkins, H., Jr. "Risk Manager." *Wall Street Journal*, March 3–4, 2007, A9.

10. Corcoran, E. "Intel Plots a Comeback." *Forbes*, June 4, 2007, 92.

11. Schuler, A. "Overcoming Resistance to Change: Top Ten Reasons for Change Resistance." *www.SchulerSolutions.com* (2003). Retrieved June 27, 2008, from http://www.schulersolutions.com/resistance_to_change .html.

12. Fahey, J. "Can This Brand Be Saved?" *Forbes* (Mar. 29, 2004). Retrieved June 26, 2008, from http://www.forbes.com/global/2004/0329/044.html.

13. Ibid.

14. Hammons, K. H. "No Risk, No Reward." *Fast Company* (Mar. 2002, issue 57). Retrieved June 26, 2008, from http://www.fastcompany.com/ magazine/57/riskreward.html.

15. See note 12.

16. Carty, S. S. "GM to Start Loan Blitz for '04 Models." *Wall Street Journal*, Sept. 22, 2004, A3.

17. Trottman, M. "As Competition Rebounds, Southwest Faces Squeeze." *Wall Street Journal*, June 27, 2007, A1.

18. Ibid.

19. Frazier, M. "Geico's Big Spending Pays Off, Study Says." *Advertising Age* (June 26, 2007). Retrieved July 5, 2007, from http://adage.com/abstract .php?article_id=118844.

20. Brooks, R. "Krispy Kreme's Profit Plunges 56%." *Wall Street Journal*, Aug. 27, 2004, A3.

21. "Growth Companies—The World's Top 200." (n.d.). Retrieved June 26, 2008, from www.deloitte.com/top200/leverage/htm.

22. Russell, J. "Glaxo Looks to R&D Cure for Falling Profits." *Telegraph* (July 25, 2008). Retrieved Aug. 22, 2008, from http://www.telegraph.co.uk/money/main.jhtml?xml=/money/2008/07/24/cngsk124.xml.

23. Pietz, J. "Moto to Cut Jobs from R&D Unit." *Crain's Chicago Business* (June 12, 2008). Retrieved Aug. 22, 2008, from http://www.chicago business.com/cgi-bin/news.pl?id=29800.

24. See note 21.

25. "Coke and Marlboro Man Voted 20th Century's Brand Heroes." *Marketing* (Nov. 25, 1999). Retrieved Oct. 10, 2008, from http://www.brandrepublic .com/Marketing/News/69452/.

26. Terhune, C. "Coke Investors Crave Dramatic Fix from CEO." *Wall Street Journal*, Sept. 22, 2004, C1.

27. "Sustaining Corporate Growth Requires 'Big I' and 'Small I' Innovation." *Knowledge@Wharton* (Feb. 21, 2007). Retrieved Feb. 28, 2007, from http://knowledge.wharton.upenn.edu/article.cfm?articleid=1662&cf.

Chapter 7

1. Mullman, J. "Miller Genuinely Daft: Changes Its Message—Again." *Advertising Age*, Apr. 7, 2008, 1.

2. Kesmodel, D. "Sales Clouds Brewing for 'Vacation in a Bottle.'" *Wall Street Journal*, Apr. 3, 2008, B1.

3. UCSF Library, Tobacco Videos. "Joe Cullman: The History of Marlboro" (1995) [video]. *Internet Archive* (June 16, 2006). Retrieved June 20, 2008, from http://www.archive.org/details/typ23e00.

4. "Financial Information." *Philip Morris USA* (n.d.). Retrieved June 21, 2008, from http://philipmorrisusa.com/en/cms/Company/Financial_Information/default.aspx.

5. Edmonds, S., and Nordenstam, S. "Absolut Vodka Gaining U.S. Market Share-CEO." *Reuters* (Mar. 14, 2007). Retrieved June 23, 2008, from http://www.reuters.com/article/mergersNews/idUSL1444696220070314.

6. Capell, K. "Absolut Makeover." *BusinessWeek* (Jan. 16, 2006). Retrieved June 23, 2008, from http://www.businessweek.com/bwdaily/dnflash/jan2006/nf20060116_1577_db039.htm.

7. "FedEx Corporation Annual Report 2007." *FedEx.com* (n.d.). Retrieved June 21, 2008, from http://www.fedex.com/us/investorrelations/financial info/2007annualreport/online.

8. "Jack in the Box—About Our Company." (n.d.). Retrieved June 23, 2008, from http://www.jackinthebox.com/aboutourco/history.php.

9. Rauwald, C. "BMW Widens Its Sales Lead over Rivals." *Wall Street Journal*, June 9, 2008, B2.

10. Miller, S. "BMW Bucks Diversification to Focus on Luxury Models." *Wall Street Journal*, Mar. 20, 2002, B4.

11. Breen, B. "Driven by Design." *Fast Company,* Sept. 2002, 123.

12. "The Ultimate Brand?" *Wall Street Journal,* Dec. 4, 2000, C26.

13. Lienert, P., and Krebs, M. "The Boss at BMW: Q&A with Helmut Panke." *Edmunds* (Nov. 10, 2005). Retrieved June 23, 2008, from http://www.edmunds.com/insideline/do/Features/articleId=107803.

14. Hudson, K. "Pier 1 Plots Sales Turnaround." *Wall Street Journal,* Aug. 2, 2005, B7.

15. Williamson, R. "Pier 1 Tries 'New Attitude' with Loomis." *Adweek* (Mar. 22, 2006). Retrieved June 23, 2008, from http://www.adweek.com/aw/research/article_display.jsp?vnu_content_id=1002234253.

16. "The Good News . . . and the Bad News." *Wall Street Journal,* June 10, 2008, C6.

17. "Pier 1 Imports®—Press Releases" (Apr. 10, 2008). Retrieved June 23, 2008, from http://www.pier1.com/SideMenu/IR/PressRelease/tabid/94/default.aspx?ReleaseID=1127867.

18. Alsop, R. "Scandal-Filled Year Takes Toll on Companies' Good Names." *Wall Street Journal,* Feb. 12, 2003, B1.

19. Dolan, M., and Spector, M. "Ford Aims to Wow Key Group: Its Dealers." *Wall Street Journal,* Apr. 14, 2008, B8.

20. Taylor, E., and Valcourt, J. "Daimler Sheds Light on Chrysler." *Wall Street Journal,* Feb. 28, 2008, A1.

21. Kiley, D. "Brand New Day: Why CMO Tenures Are So Short." *BusinessWeek* (June 20, 2006). Retrieved June 23, 2008, from http://www.businessweek.com/the_thread/brandnewday/archives/2006/06/why_cmo_tenures.html?chan=search.

22. Felicelli, M. "2007 Route to the Top." *SpencerStuart* (Nov. 1, 2007). Retrieved June 23, 2008, from content.spencerstuart.com/sswebsite/pdf/lib/Final_Summary_for_2008_publication.pdf#nameddest=Tenure.

23. Landers, P. "Sharp Covets the Sony Model: A Sexy, High-End Image." *Wall Street Journal,* Mar. 11, 2002, A13.

Chapter 8

1. Neuborne, E. "Stung by Slow Sales, Zippo Turns to Brand Extensions." *Inc.com* (Sept. 1, 2001). Retrieved June 24, 2008, from http://www.inc.com/magazine/20040901/casestudy.html.

2. Hanessian, B. and Sierra, C. "Leading a Turnaround: An Interview with the Chairman of D&B." *McKinsey Quarterly,* May 2005, 2.

3. Ibid.

4. "New World Restaurant Group Launches Einstein Bros. Cafe [Press Releases]." (Oct. 14, 2004). Retrieved Oct. 10, 2008, from http://phx.corporate-ir.net/phoenix.zhtml?c=177910&p=irol-newsArticle&ID=642783&highlight.

5. Ibid.

6. Moore, P. "Einstein Bros. Bagels Rebranding." *Denver Business Journal* (Oct. 14, 2004). Retrieved June 24, 2008, from http://www.bizjournals .com/denver/s.
7. "Einstein Noah Restaurant Group Reports Solid Growth in Revenue, Comparable Store Sales and Net Income." (Feb. 27, 2008). Retrieved Oct. 10, 2008, from http://phx.corporate-ir.net/phoenix.zhtml?c =177910&p=irol-newsArticle&ID=1113223&highlight.

Chapter 9

1. "Army Leadership—Competent, Confident, and Agile." *Scribd* (Oct. 12, 2006). Retrieved June 23, 2008, from http://www.scribd.com/doc/ 2472102/Army-fm6-22-Army-Leadership.
2. Adamy, J. "Peltz Stirs Things Up at Starbucks." *Wall Street Journal*, May 17–18, 2008, A3.
3. "Peter F. Drucker Quotes." *BrainyQuote* (n.d.). Retrieved June 23, 2008, from http://www.brainyquote.com/quotes/authors/p/peter_f_drucker.html.
4. Landler, M. "Buffett's Shopping Trip to Europe Draws a Crowd." *New York Times* (May 20, 2008). Retrieved June 23, 2008, from http://www.nytimes .com/2008/05/20/business/worldbusiness/20buffett.html.
5. Linder, J. C. "Continuous Renewal: Managing for the Upside." *Accenture* (June 2005). Retrieved June 23, 2008, from http://www.accenture.com/ Global/Research_and_Insights/Outlook/ContinuousUpside.htm.
6. Ibid.

Chapter 10

1. "Corporate Information: Google Company Overview." (n.d.). Retrieved June 27, 2008, from http://www.google.com/intl/en/corporate.
2. "Peter F. Drucker Quotes." *Thinkexist.com* (n.d.). Retrieved June 27, 2008, from http://thinkexist.com/quotation/the_aim_of_marketing_is_to _know_and_understand/321855.html.
3. Gudder, S. "Math Quotes, Sayings About Mathematics." *The Quote Garden* (n.d.). Retrieved June 24, 2008, from http://www.quotegarden.com/ math.html.

Chapter 11

1. Stringer, K. "Hard Lesson Learned: Premium and No-Frills Don't Mix." *Wall Street Journal*, Nov. 3, 2003, B1.
2. "Men Buy, Women Shop: The Sexes Have Different Priorities When Walking Down the Aisles." *Knowledge@Wharton* (Nov. 28, 2007). Retrieved June 24, 2008, from http://www.upenn.edu/researchatpenn/ article.php?1330&bus.

3. Elliott, S. "Research Finds Consumers Worldwide Belong to Six Basic Groups That Cross National Lines." *New York Times* (June 25, 1998). Retrieved June 24, 2008, from http://query.nytimes.com/gst/fullpage .html?res=9403E3D9113CF936A15755C0A96E958260.

4. "What Kind of Driver Are You?" *Audi Enthusiast Magazine*, n.d., p. 54.

5. Merrill, C. "A Mother's Work Is Never Done?" *American Demographics*, Sept. 1999, 29.

6. Porter, M. "What Is Strategy?" *Harvard Business Review*, Nov.–Dec. 1996, 61.

7. Zook, C. "Finding Your Next Core Business." *Harvard Business Review*, Apr. 2007, 8.

8. Breen, B. "Practice Your Storytelling." *Fast Company*, Mar. 2005, 67.

9. Taylor, A., III. "Seven and the Dwarf." *Fortune*, Apr. 15, 2002, 386.

10. "Be Careful About Whom You Serve." *Fast Company*, Mar. 2005, 66.

11. *Brill's Content*, Feb. 1, 1999, 95.

12. Walley, W. "Fox News Sweeps to TV Marketer of the Year." *Advertising Age*, Nov. 4, 2002, 1.

13. O'Connell, V. "Is Discount a Good Fit for Vera Wang?" *Wall Street Journal*, Sept. 5, 2007, B1.

14. "Ticker." *Brill's Content*, Feb. 1999, 128.

15. "Purpose, Values and Principles." *PG.com* (n.d.). Retrieved June 27, 2008, from http://www.pg.com/company/who_we_are/ppv.jhtml.

16. Knudsen, T. "Escaping the Middle-Market Trap: An Interview with the CEO of Electrolux." *McKinsey Quarterly*, 2006, 4, 29.

17. Ohmae, K. "Getting Back to Strategy." *Harvard Business Review*, 1988, 66(6), 149–156.

18. Passikoff, R. "Let's Move Research into the 21st Century." *Revolution*, Mar. 2000, 45.

19. Silver, S. "How Match.com Found Love Among Boomers." *Wall Street Journal*, Jan. 27, 2007, A1.

20. Vascellaro, J. "Ask Searches for Answer to Luring New Users." *Wall Street Journal*, Jan. 25, 2008, B1.

21. Vascellaro, J. "What Is Ask.com's New Strategy?" *Wall Street Journal*, Mar. 5, 2008, B3.

22. Adamy, J. "Man Behind Burger King Turnaround." *Wall Street Journal*, Apr. 2, 2008, B1.

23. See note 6.

24. Hyashi, A. "When to Trust Your Gut." *Harvard Business Review* (Feb. 2001). Retrieved June 26, 2008, from http://www.hbsp.harvard.edu/hbsp/ hbr/articles/article.jsp?articleID=R0102C&ml_action=get-article&page Number=1&ml_subscriber=true&referral=2533.

25. Ingrassia, P. "Can Bob Lutz Shake GM Out of Its Stupor?" *Wall Street Journal*, Aug. 7, 2001, A14.

26. Tucker, C. "Making the Brand." *Southwest Airlines Spirit*, Mar. 2002, 34.

27. Underhill, R. W. "Who's Minding the Brand?" *Arthur Anderson Retailing Issues Letter,* July 1999, 11(4), 1.
28. Shirouzu, N. "This Is Not Your Father's Toyota." *Wall Street Journal,* Mar. 26, 2002, B1.
29. Ibid.
30. Shirouzu, N. "Scion Plays Hip-Hop Impresario to Impress Young Drivers." *Wall Street Journal,* Oct. 5, 2004, B1.

Chapter 12

1. Porter, M. "What Is Strategy?" *Harvard Business Review,* Nov.–Dec. 1996, 62.
2. Christensen, C., Cook, S., and Hall, T. "It's the Purpose Brand, Stupid." *Wall Street Journal,* Nov. 29, 2005, B2.
3. See note 1, 61.
4. Welch, J., and Welch, S. *Winning.* New York: HarperCollins, 2005.
5. See note 1, 61.
6. From internal newsletters by David C. Baker, ReCourses, Inc., http://www.resourses.com.
7. Ibid.
8. *Fast Company Fast Take Newsletter,* July 17, 2002.
9. "How Citi Is Organized." (n.d.). Retrieved June 24, 2008, from http://www.citigroup.com/citigroup/business/index.htm.
10. "In Search of Growth." *Wall Street Journal,* June 9, 2008, R3.
11. Adamson, A. *BrandSimple.* New York: Palgrave Macmillan, 2006, 111.
12. Lautman, M. "The ABC's of Positioning." *Marketing Research,* Winter 1993, 18.
13. Anders, G. "Founders' Hubris Fuels Corporate Drama." *Wall Street Journal,* June 4, 2008, B2.
14. Jeff Goodby, co-chair, Goodby Silverstein & Partners, in an *Advertising Age* mailer. Holt, D. "Got Milk?" AEF [Advertising Educational Foundation] (2002). Retrieved June 27, 2008, from http://www.aef.com/on_campus/classroom/case_histories/3000.
15. Gremillion, J. "The Big Leap." *Adweek,* Mar. 18, 1999, 58.
16. Gatorade Sports Science Institute. "Overview." (n.d.). Retrieved June 24, 2008, from http://www.gssiweb.com/History_GSSI.aspx?ExpandMenu=6.
17. Vranica, S. "Agency's Work for PepsiCo Fizzles Out." *Wall Street Journal,* Apr. 17, 2008, B9.
18. "Welcome to K-BOB's Steakhouse" (n.d.). Retrieved June 24, 2008, from http://www.kbobs.com/about.html.
19. Rayburn, R. "Ritz-Carlton Found the Key." *Albuquerque Journal,* Feb. 28, 2002, 2.
20. "The Ultimate Brand?" *Wall Street Journal,* Dec. 4, 2000, C26.
21. Caggiano, C. "Everything I Know I Learned from Warren Buffet." *Inc.com,* July 1999, 85.
22. Ibid.

Chapter 13

1. "What Makes Crystal Springs So Good?" (n.d.). Retrieved June 24, 2008, from http://www.crystalh2o.com/companyinfo.html.
2. Murrow, E. R. "Language Quotes and Sayings." *Quote Garden* (n.d.). Retrieved June 26, 2008, from http://www.quotegarden.com/language.html.
3. Hurd, M. "The UnCarly." *Forbes*, Mar. 12, 2007, 83.
4. Ibid.
5. Scheck, J. "PC Demand Boots HP Profit." *Wall Street Journal*, Feb. 20, 2008, A3.
6. Byron, E. "Sale of Neiman's Is Latest Sign of Luxury Halo." *Wall Street Journal*, May 3, 2005, B1.
7. Hammonds, K. "Big Bets, Fast Failures." *Fast Company* (June 1, 2001). Retrieved Oct. 10, 2008, from http://www.fastcompany.com/articles/2001/07/nadler.html.
8. Porter, M. "What Is Strategy?" *Harvard Business Review*, Nov.–Dec. 1996, 61.
9. Ibid.
10. Zimmerman, A., and Lloyd, M. E. "Home Depot Net Falls 66% as Store Growth Breaks." *Wall Street Journal*, May 21, 2008, B3.
11. Zimmerman, A. "Home Depot Chief Renovates." *Wall Street Journal*, June 5, 2008, B1.
12. Ibid.
13. "Fees Don't Fly with Us." *Wall Street Journal*, June 3, 2008, A5.
14. Baca, A. "Grove: Intel Back on Track." *Albuquerque Journal*, Oct. 16, 1998, A1.
15. Freeman, L. "Business-to-Business Advertisers Top 100." *Business Marketing*, Sept. 1997.
16. Larsen, P. F. "Better Is . . . Better." *Wall Street Journal*, Sept. 22, 2003, R6.
17. See note 11.

Chapter 14

1. Gladwell, Malcolm. *The Tipping Point*. Back Bay Books, 2002, and *Blink*. Back Bay Books, 2007; Gilmore, James. *The Experience Economy*. Harvard Business School Press, 1999; and Pink, Daniel. *A Whole New Mind*. Riverhead Hardcover, 2005.
2. Sanders, J. O., *Spiritual Leadership*. Chicago: Moody, 1989.
3. "Newspapers Will Be an Endangered Species Unless They Embrace the Web and Ever-More Targeted Communities." *Brill's Content*, July–Aug. 1999, 111.

About the Author

Steve McKee is the president and cofounder of McKee Wallwork Cleveland, a full-service marketing communications firm that has twice been awarded the American Marketing Association's Effie Award, one of the industry's highest honors. He learned his craft working at a handful of some of the best-known advertising agencies in the world, including NW Ayer, Della Femina, and a division of McCann-Erickson Worldwide.

Steve has been published or quoted in the *New York Times*, *USA Today*, *Advertising Age*, *Adweek*, *Investor's Business Daily*, and the *Los Angeles Times*, as well as in dozens of regional and local newspapers and magazines throughout the United States. He has appeared on CNBC, ESPN2, CNNfn, Bloomberg radio, and network television affiliates in two dozen cities across America. He currently writes a monthly advertising advice column for *BusinessWeek.com*.

Steve is a popular speaker and has shared his insights with organizations that include British Airways, Einstein Bros. Bagels, the American Marketing Association, Grant Thornton Executive Seminars, the Society for Marketing Professional Services, the Frequent Travel Marketing Association, and the International Executive MBA Council, among others.

Steve lives with his wife and children in beautiful Albuquerque, New Mexico, his adopted hometown. He welcomes reader feedback at SMcKee@WhenGrowthStalls.com.

Index